CREATING

A

LINE FAMILY

CREATING
A
LINE FAMILY

LOVE,
ABUNDANCE
AND BELONGING
IN THE NEW MILLENIUM

Richard Gilmore
and Elon de Arcana

*Author's
Initial
Printing*

ISBN—10: 0692457968
ISBN—13: 978-0692457962

Dedication:

This book is dedicated to our supportive poly family partners Judy and Jim. Thank you for all of your understanding and following us through the lava flows on Hawaii. We love you.

Confidential to RH, if you made it, please come back and get us.

Acknowledgements:

We didn't build this all by ourselves. First we would like to thank Guttenberg for making the concept of mass market books possible.

Wow, this list is full of generous and loving people. The list has to start with Tamara and Doug who asked us intelligent questions about the line family concept. This book is our attempt at intelligent answers to those questions. Once we got going all sorts of great people helped in large and small ways. These include (in no particular order): Anita, Lightfoot, Woosi, Meghan & Mark, Robyn & Chewy, Vashti & Leon, Nicole, Alan, Quintus, all the long-term poly families we interviewed, the intentional communities on the Big Island and around the country, Benjamin and the Windward line family (especially Walt, Lindsay, Andrew & Opalyn).

We are also grateful to the organizations that have let us put on our line family presentation; Polycamp NW, Westercon, V-Con, Rusty Con, Spo-Con, the Forum group in Kihei, Loving More Poly Retreat, Poly Living Convention Philadelphia, Polycon Denver and Polycon Vancouver BC.

We thank Christopher Bingham and Bone Poets Orchestra for the use of the song Three in our presentations and on the website www.line-family.info. Check out Bone Poets Orchestra music at http://www.bonepoets.com/.

We know we have forgotten someone and we are terribly sorry. We love you too.

Legal disclaimer:

We are not attorneys. We repeat that several times in the book. To the best of our knowledge the legal references in this book were correct at the time that we wrote the book. However, some may have been wrong and others may now be out-of-date. Laws change, become outdated or are ruled invalid. Courts sometimes interpret laws more broadly (see Citizens United for example). These are some of the reasons you need an attorney instead of relying on what you find in this book.

All we have done is attempted to let you know about some – not all – of the legal tools available to you and your line family. One of the attorneys we talked to said it best, "An attorney helps people do what they want to do and a good attorney keeps you out of court." Yes, an attorney is expensive, but not nearly as expensive as not having one.

A positive attitude may not solve all your problems, but it will annoy enough people to make it worth the effort!

Herm Albright

If there is a book that you want to read, but it hasn't been written yet, you must be the one to write it.

Toni Morrison

Patience

In our current culture patience is not a popular concept. We have become used to electronic communications over writing a letter by hand. We have movies streamed into our homes rather than waiting for it to show up on our TV schedule. We order the latest gadget as soon as possible online instead of checking it out in a store or waiting for reviews. I do all those things. It is not intrinsically bad, it just sets us up to lose patience with slower processes.

But patience is powerful, not passive (unless all you do is sit around complaining). Patience is powerful when you have a well-defined goal to work towards. Most people who have started a successful small business will tell you about the patience it took to get the business to where it was turning a profit. And then it takes more time to pay back the initial investment your family made in supporting you and the new business. But a successful business can grow and provide family members with employment and the family portfolio with steady income.

Patience is also powerful in investing. It is generally a good idea to have a diversified portfolio to limit your risk. If you choose to own individual stocks, invest in companies that produce goods or services you are familiar with (it worked for me when I bought my Apple stock in 2001). Only sell an investment when there is a compelling reason. It is truly amazing how many people sell at the bottom of a market and buy at the top. Patience will help you avoid that trap.

The ultimate patience is working for a goal that you realize might not be accomplished in your lifetime. Your fledgling line family may not reach all the goals you have envisioned for it during your lifetime. That was true of the United States founding fathers. It did not stop them. Their concern was for "posterity" a word they used often to indicate that their vision was for the generations to follow. That is when you enter the realm of true visionaries of social reform such as Martin Luther King Jr. and Mahatma Gandhi who sowed the seeds of cultural change.

A Little History

History is full of groups using line family concepts. Monks and nuns are classic examples of families that continue without end by adding new young members. Of course these examples are of the single-sex line family model. Organized crime has used the line family model to keep their "families" going through many generations.

Even in the short history of the United States families play a pivotal role in business and politics. We have had two sets of father/son presidents and one grandfather/grandson presidential pair. As we write this book a second son of a presidential father (and brother of a previous president) has announced that he is a presidential candidate for 2016. With the announcement that Hillary Clinton is running, we now also have a possible husband/wife presidential pair. The Muhlenberg family was in political life from the revolutionary war until 1980. It makes the Kennedy family's 64 years in politics seem short.

History also shows us that line families are a time-tested way to create and keep wealth, power and influence. When you look behind the trappings of power in churches, royalty, governments and especially businesses, you find the structure of family. Corporations are artificial persons, but they are run by real people. Quite often the top management and/or owners are families that are hidden behind trusts, shell companies and other legal tools used to manage wealth.

What constitutes wealth? Many might answer money. They are not wrong, but money is not the complete answer. Money can pay for shelter, clothing, food, vehicles and hospital bills. Money may not buy happiness, but happiness is a lot closer at hand when you are not worried about where your next meal is coming from. Security is a large part of what wealth means to me. When I am both secure in my basic needs and know that I have the means to pursue my interests, I am happy, or at least content with my life. Money is a powerful tool and has a role in satisfying basic needs. We talk about money a fair amount in this book.

Other kinds of wealth show up in my life. I recently had severe medical problems. Fortunately I was able to have two of my three family members watch over me while I was in the hospital. The presence of loving and concerned family members made me feel wealthy indeed and helped me to recover quickly.

The Main Message

If nothing else, we are here to tell you one thing - families are the most powerful social, political and economic organizations on Earth... except for the "nuclear family."

Can I back up that statement? Yes I can. I have already mentioned multi-generational, political families. Let's take a look at economics. Examples of the economic power of families can be found in U.S. business statistics. For example, in 2011 there were 5.5 million family businesses. These businesses contributed 57% of the U.S. GDP (that's $8.3 trillion). Family businesses also employed 63% of the workforce (FEUSA, 2011). In 2006 over one third (35%) of Fortune 500 companies were owned or controlled by families (Business Week 2006). Many of these businesses are multigenerational or have plans for younger family members to take over the business. Family owned businesses have longevity. The average lifespan for a family business is 24 years. The average lifespan for an S&P 500 company is around 15 years. If you take family owned businesses out of the calculation, the average lifespan for the remaining S&P 500 companies would be even shorter.

Family businesses lead changes in the social area as well. In 2007, Fortune Magazine reported that 24% of family owned businesses were led by a female CEO or president and 33% had a woman slated to take over the business when the current management retires. Also in 2007 the Mass Mutual Family Business Survey reported that around 60% of family businesses had women in top management positions. This is particularly interesting considering the fact that women led only 2.5% of Fortune 1000 companies in 2007. In September of 2014, the percentage of female CEOs and presidents had climbed to 5.3%. The trend is slow, but we think it's good and that it is being led by family businesses.

Nuclear families are hobbled by not understanding how to build wealth and security over multiple generations. We will explain how a lot of estate planning advice seems designed to keep low- and middle-class families low and middle class. Even if you don't fully accept the line family concept, we hope that you can benefit from using some of the tools mentioned in this book and that subsequent generations will remember you as the founder of family prosperity and wellbeing.

Be aware that there are no "get-rich-quick" schemes in this book. It is extremely unlikely that anyone can grow a line family of 20 members in just a few years. It will likely take decades – as will the building of a substantial portfolio. So time's a wasting, we suggest that you get started now.

In Closing

We hope that in at least some small way this book will cause a ripple or two that will help change the current power imbalance in society. People need to have control in their lives, free from the fear of hunger, homelessness, disease and isolation. As President Roosevelt stated in the January 11, 1944 State of the Union address, "We have come to a clear realization of the fact that true individual freedom cannot exist without economic security and independence. 'Necessitous men are not free men.' People who are hungry and out of a job are the stuff of which dictatorships are made."

Grandiose stuff for a little book? Perhaps it is. But if you're going to dream, dream big. As for you gentle reader, take what you will from this book and leave the rest to ponder another day. We humbly thank you for taking the time (your most precious and valuable possession) to read and consider our ideas. Let me end with a quote from a wonderful philosopher, "If you obey all the rules, you miss all the fun." – Katharine Hepburn

If you have any questions or suggestions, or want to book a presentation, please contact us at: director@line-family.info.

Blessings and joy to you, your family and your community.

The more you love the more you can love, and the more intensely you love. Nor is there any limit on how many you can love. If a person had time enough he could love all of that majority who are decent and just.

Lazarus Long (in "Time Enough for Love")

Life is meant to be lived,
not looked at from a distance.

Sofie Kelly

As I was growing up I often wondered why it was that every family on the block had to have their own lawnmower, shovels, rakes, etc. After all we were usually not all doing the same sort of projects at the same time, so it would be easy to share them. But that didn't seem to be the way the world worked. I wondered why then, and I still do. Our society seems to require that we all buy things continuously in order for the economy to keep moving. What if we started sharing with our neighbors? Or if we created a large family of like-minded people and shared with each other? And we can share love too, not just things, much more freely than our society seems to think is acceptable. I think that it is time for people to realize that it up to them to choose how they invest their time, money and love. Invest love? Indeed! Well invested it has very high returns!

Have you ever wondered how many family members and/or friends you would need in order to have someone to do a certain activity with you? I have, and do. The first time it happened I had a husband and a boyfriend and no one with whom to go to a New Year's Eve party. Don't get me wrong - it's not that I don't like doing things by myself. In 2000, just before I started dating Richard, I went "drive about" by myself for 4+ weeks. And given the time and resources I'd gladly do it again. I'm a person who not only enjoys their own company, but requires time alone now and then. But not all the time! And not when there is something that I want to do, but not by myself. Parties tend to fit into that category, on those occasions when going to a party sounds good to me. I love having family around, the more the merrier, until I need to be alone for a while. Meeting new people appeals to me too, though I'm much more introverted than Richard is. When there is a project to be done you can count me in, as long as I don't have to do it alone. Teamwork makes everything more fun for me!

How about you? Are you interested in the idea of gathering together a family group that will continue for generations? Would you like to have a multi-generational family that supports you in what you'd like to do with your life - financially, emotionally and physically? If so, this book could be very helpful for you. It will not tell you how to gather the people, but rather it suggests things to consider doing as you gather your family and beyond. Perhaps you are, or want to be, part of an intentional community that does not encourage polyamory. Maybe you want to always live alone, but to be connected with other people. Or maybe you are monogamous and want to be, or already are, part of a nuclear family - with or without the standard 2.5 children. It really doesn't matter. We have gathered information for this book that is valuable regardless of your love/relationship style. I hope you will find it interesting and useful!

Richard and I attempted to make the chapters of this book as factual and opinion-free as we could. As I was reviewing the chapters I found that I had some definite opinions about the topics. We decided that it would be acceptable for me to add those at the end of the chapters. They are my opinions, not facts, but I hope they will inspire you to think about how the information in the chapters fits into your life and your family's plans and dreams.

Access to the Book's Companion Website

Creating a Line Family references the laws of many states. The problem is that state laws change. New laws are created, courts make precedent setting decisions and local jurisdictions add to state laws.

We have created a companion website to try and keep up with laws that affect non-monogamous households. We hope that you will help us to keep the website current. Please let us know about pending or actual changes in the laws of your state or locality that might affect a multi-partner family. Together we hope to make this a valuable resource.

On the book's companion website you will find all of the Internet address links we refer to in the book. They are listed in order by chapter. Links to additional legal materials and other related information are also found on the companion website.

Use the following information to log on:

website:	www.line-family.info/CALF_companion/
user name:	Wandering
password:	notLost

Send your updates and comments for the website to: director@line-family.info

CONTENTS

What is a Line Family?

In order to ask a question,
one must already know part of the answer.

Phoebe S. Spinrad

You are holding a book about something new that is actually quite old; line families. Robert Heinlein coined the term "line marriage" in his 1966 book; The Moon is A Harsh Mistress. In his story, the Moon is a penal colony. There is a 2-to-1 ratio of males to females. This imbalance is the main reason a new type of social norm develops in this dangerous and isolated environment. Heinlein uses the severe gender imbalance to explain the origin of this non-monogamous relationship style. Science fiction lets authors get away with almost anything; however, this is not a science fiction book. This book is based on history and science. Also we will not be using the term "marriage" as is tends to disrupt the discussion with conversations about the meaning of marriage and its religious connections.

Line Family Definition

For our purposes we will use the following definition:

line family

n

1. (Sociology) A family that continues indefinitely by adding new, generally younger, spouses of both sexes over time.

What would the definition be of a perfect line family? If we knew that this book would be much shorter. We're not sure there is such a thing as a perfect line family, intentional community or monogamous marriage. As people age, they learn new things about themselves and the world. We often hear that a couple separated or divorced because they grew apart. We think that is a lovely turn of phrase. The idea of growing apart casts no blame and assigns no guilt or shame. Growth often happens in small steps, tiny increments that are individually hard to notice. Then, after a period of time, differences become obvious and changes in circumstances must be made in order to be true to yourself. Some might call this selfish, but is it? When two people are no longer sharing a life because of growing differences they simply become roommates. If this happens, it is a cause for revisiting your agreements with a partner or partners.

According to Dan of the Dragonfyre Circle intentional community, there is something similar that happens in communities with some regularity. "In my experience it seems that every two or three years a major decision is made or a natural event occurs that causes people to rethink their relationship to a community. People who no longer feel in tune with their community will leave. A decision to leave can happen over the course of a month or two or, in extreme circumstances, it can happen overnight.

Quite a few years ago I was in a community located in a forested area on the east coast of the US. Physically it was a very nice place. Members of the community, over several years of hard work, had built all of the buildings on the land. The cabins were comfortable throughout the year and the common buildings were well designed for community gatherings with a well-appointed kitchen. When the community was about 10 years old a forest fire burned down about 90% of the buildings. Thirty percent of the people left the next day. Maybe they viewed the community as the physical spaces that they had helped to build. Perhaps some felt it was a dangerous place to stay. It just seemed that their ties to the infrastructure were stronger than their ties to the other community members and the community ideals."

We can say with some certainty that your line family will occasionally have members who feel the need to leave. Our lives go through seasons and our needs change. Sometimes our needs change radically and we find ourselves on a different path. Sometimes we discover that where we are is not where we thought we were. People can grow apart from their partners, communities and line families without it being anybody's fault.

We feel that people who practice responsible non-monogamy are well suited to the line family concept. Non-monogamous people must be able to communicate clearly with all of the people with whom they are in relationship. Clear, honest and compassionate communication is enhanced when people are open to really hearing what is being said to them and by being able to speak their truth. Being able to negotiate rather than confront is another trait we see in successful multi-adult families. Disagreements and misunderstandings do occur; however, people in successful non-monogamous relationships have developed or learned skills for handling these situations. One skill we strongly recommend learning is Non-Violent Communication. There are many books and classes on the subject. Those and other communication skills bring stability to a family and are one of the things that make a line family possible.

What You Will Find in this Book

This is a book of tools, not rules. We are offering you some of the tools you might need to build your own line family. We have attempted to be as practical as possible. Much of what you will find here has been known by the upper classes for centuries. We will explore some of those "different rules" that the rich and powerful live by. We want you to have the potential for greater economic security. We want your elder family members to have a secure retirement in a loving home surrounded by people who care about them. We want your children to get a secure start in life with a good education and no burdensome debt.

Chapter 1, Intimacy explores the breadth and depth of human intimacies. Because the topic of sex is covered by countless writers, researchers and philosophers, we spend very little time on the subject. Our focus is on other types of intimacies. These include emotional, intellectual, spiritual, nonsexual touch, financial, creative and recreational intimacies. We see intimacy as part of the social glue that can lead to a stable line family.

Chapter 2, Capital is about more than just money. While money is part of the definition of capital, we look at other types of capital that are of value to a line family. Biological capital is the value of being young and having the potential to develop skills and acquire knowledge relevant to a changing culture and advancing technology. Intellectual capital is life experience and formal education. Track record is the proven ability to complete projects whether they are personal endeavors or organizing and leading people in accomplishing a task. Social capital is often measured by who you know and an ability to make connections with influential people. Cultural capital is more about the knowledge and experience of various social groups.

Chapter 3, Vision and Agreements covers the related topics of the overall vision of a line family and its agreements. A line family vision is what your members are passionate about and the broad goals you set. Agreements are the details of how the family interacts with each other and the world outside the family.

Chapter 4, Household Management describes actual examples of how a cohousing group and some long-term polyamorous families handle the day-to-day tasks required for living together. These are examples from which your line family could develop concepts for managing a household.

Chapter 5, Finances looks at some of the tools and legal issues around finances. We look at the shortcomings of wills, the use of trusts and powers of attorney. We also review some investment strategies for building a family portfolio and introduce a few concepts about creating family businesses.

Chapter 6, Children reviews some of the social, financial and legal issues around children born into a line family. Birthrate control is discussed, as is the need for child protection plans and funding strategies for a child's education.

Chapter 7, Family Decision Making details many techniques a line family can use for group decision making. We also look at some of the unforeseen problems that crop up when using an inappropriate decision-making tool for a given situation.

Chapter 8, Owning Real Property looks at a variety of methods a line family can use to own real property. We review legal tools suited for owning a family's primary residence. We also discuss the different methods of ownership and control required for income-producing real estate.

Chapter 9, Homestead Skills for Urban & Suburban Dwellers describes tools that might seem more appropriate for rural line families, but are also suited to suburban and even urban living.

Chapter 10, Random Notes shares topics that we wanted in the book; however, they really didn't fit in any of the other chapters. In this chapter you will find some history, a little magic, how to plan for the unexpected and more.

Chapter 11, Cohabitation Arrangements looks at state laws and how they affect an unmarried couple's relationship. There are also plenty of laws that can negatively impact a multi-adult family. We discuss ways to mitigate the negative effects of many laws. We also describe a set of laws that can be used to create a workable, legal framework for your line family.

Chapter 12, The Windward Line Family was co-written with the help of an actual line family that has been together since 1980. The Windward line family lives in a rural setting in south central Washington State. Members of the family answer questions and comment about living as a line family. We were thrilled to find this family while doing research for the book. It is nice to know there is at least one group making this work. We suspect that there are others whom we have not yet discovered.

What You Won't Find in this Book

We assume that ethical non-monogamy, sometimes called polyamory, works. We've been in a MFFM quad since late 2000. We will not be talking about jealousy, sexual practices or where to find dates. There are a lot of websites and books for those issues.

We hope you will find useful information in this book whether you are trying to form a line family or just want suggestions for day-to-day issues affecting non-monogamous families. If you have any questions or suggestions, or want to book a presentation by us on this topic, please contact us at: director@line-family.info.

Blessings and joy to you, your family and your community. Richard, Elon and the Nonesuch Family

CHAPTER ONE

Intimacy

*You never change things by fighting the existing reality.
To change something, build a new model that makes
the existing model obsolete.*

R. Buckminster Fuller

*I have often heard it said that 'You can't live on love' or
that 'Love is not enough'. What if the problem is that
society's definition of love is not enough?*

Richard Gilmore

Types of Intimacy

Here's a word association test. We say intimacy, you say...? Sex? It's what
most people past puberty seem to say, and that's alright. But let's explore
other ways that people are intimate with each other. Do you have a friend
in which you confide your deepest feelings of fear and regret or hope and
joy? If you do, this must be someone that you trust very much. In turn

does this person let you into their emotional life sharing their worries and happiness? If so, this is a close friend indeed. It sounds like you know each other intimately. Is this not an intimate relationship? We think it is.

When you expand your definition of intimacy, you might start to notice intimate relationships you never thought of before. Elon has one such story:

My father is now 95 years old. He has been on his own since my mother's death in 1984, though my sister does live nearby. As a child I thought that my mother was the more socially inclined of the two of them because he was too busy working to have time for friends. Looking back I realize that he spent time socializing with people wherever he was – at his auto repair shop with customers, at parts stores and wrecking yards, with tour guides when we were on vacations – everywhere.

Now that he is retired (for 33 years) and on his own, he has a network of people that he is in contact with – mostly widows who were my mother's friends, neighbors who befriended him when my mother became ill and neighbors who were their friends and who moved away. He has had male friends also but, as so often happens, most of them have died before the female members of the same age group. He is a "jack of all trades" and often gets involved in projects to help out the women in his circle of friends, along with the help of my sister who lives next door to him. Also he often calls them, or they call him, to make plans for a meal out or a meal at one of their homes, or to come to a gathering of friends and family. Even though they are not all living in the same neighborhood, I have recently realized that they could be called an "intentional community". There certainly is plenty of companionship, looking out for each other and involvement in each other's lives. It isn't a polyamorous line family, though there is much love involved. They are not financially connected – other than helping each other out and thereby reducing the cost of getting outside help. But I would say that their group definitely has some of the best qualities of a poly line family – love, caring, fun and sharing!

Sexual Intimacy

Before we look at other intimate relationships we want to make a few comments about sex. We want to be clear on one important point. We don't think that sexual relations should be a requirement between all of the members of a line family. First, same sex relations are of interest to a minority (large minority) of people. Second, you can be intimate and in love with someone without being sexual with them. We know this from personal experience and the experiences of many other people we know.

When others first hear of the line family concept they sometimes ask, "Must the 30 somethings have sex with the 60 somethings?" Our answer is absolutely not. We feel strongly that everyone be at choice about their sexuality. As an example, we are not fans of the Kerista Commune's sex schedule where every woman slept with a different man each night. (http://www.kerista.com/ss.html). It is our opinion that all intimate relationships are unique. Some are more emotional while others are more intellectual, spiritual and/or erotic. Now on to some of the other ways, besides sex, that humans are intimate with each other.

Emotional Intimacy

Richard has some observations about men and their emotionally intimate relationships. "I have heard women make the comment that men can't or won't share their feelings. As a man I would like to make an untested observation (that means it is a guess – not a theory). I have heard it said that women tend to handle physical pain better than men. This makes sense to me because men are not designed to go through child birth; however, scientific tests show mixed results on this issue. It is my guess that women, being built differently from men, might have some ways of dealing with pain that men don't. This seems to be a reasonable biological necessity. Let's look at another reasonable biological necessity that our pre-agricultural brothers might have developed.

In hunter/gatherer groups the men are primarily the hunters and it is normally the women who do the gathering. It would seem when facing a dangerous animal with a spear or other such weapon, that overcoming fear – a strong emotion – might provide a selective advantage. If a member of the tribe was killed in the hunt, going out on subsequent hunts would be quite difficult were it not for the ability to overcome fear, doubt, anxiety, etc.

I bring up this idea only to provide a new perspective for discussion and a question: Can an innate survival trait fairly be labeled as a social deficit? It is my contention that as women handle physical pain, men handle emotional pain.

Note To Guys: You may not be too happy with the idea that women might handle pain better than you, but that's the macho talking. You try to pass a bowling ball sometime.

For the record I say that men can share emotionally intimate experiences. I have seen men together watching sports on TV. That can be an emotionally intimate experience as exhausting and socially bonding as sex. I'm not a motor-sports racing fan, but closed-track, stock car auto racing sure seems to have a large and emotional male following. My basic point is that men have emotional relationships, but they are usually not like women's emotional relationships. "

In learning about a person you have just met you will generally find out about the breadth of their life experiences and knowledge long before you get into the depth of any particular subject. As you talk with this new person, you may find you have similar passions. It seems that emotional connections are often formed around passions. As stated earlier, it might be a passion about cars or sports. Passions can also be about art such as sculpture, music or painting. One excellent definition of art that we have heard is that art provokes an emotional response to a work. A connection may be formed with a person who has similar responses to art.

Questions can come up about how a particular passion came into being. Often these are open ended questions, something like, "why does this music make you cry?" An open-ended question can – over time – be explored in greater detail. As trust and emotional intimacy grows, the answer to a question can reveal intimate details of a person's life. Generally this is not a one-sided conversation. The person who asked the question in this exchange might have a similar life experience, creating a bond between them. Or the questioner might share a totally different experience revealing more of their inner feelings. In either case, a deeper level of sharing has occurred possibly leading to a more intimate emotional relationship.

An emotionally intimate understanding of another person might lead you into being their mentor, confidant and advisor. You could be a nonjudgmental shoulder to cry on. You can celebrate their personal victories that few, if anyone else, would even understand. Of course this works both ways in a deep emotional relationship. This is the reason we think an emotionally intimate relationship by itself could be a good bond between line family members.

Intellectual Intimacy

We are willing to bet that sometime in your academic history, from elementary school to the present, you had at least one teacher with whom you clicked. Someone who saw your interest and aptitude in a subject and encouraged you to go as far as you wanted. A teacher that pushed you and you didn't care because you were both passionate about the subject. That could be considered an intellectually intimate relationship. It also happens between peers, people with similar knowledge levels that feed each other's passions. Sometimes a shared intellectual passion can push the participants to new discoveries and knowledge.

Two people that shared an intellectual passion and intimacy were the Curies. Marie Skłodowska Curie and her husband Pierre Curie shared the 1903 Nobel Prize for physics. Madam (Mrs.) Curie went on to win a second Nobel Prize for chemistry, becoming the first person to win two Nobels and the first of only two people to win Nobels in two different fields. The other winner in two fields was Linus Pauling for chemistry and peace.

Intellectual intimacy can be experienced by a mentor and student. While this relationship might seem to have a power imbalance, it has more in common with a peer relationship than a student/teacher affiliation. For one thing, the mentor does not have the power to grade, pass or fail their intellectual partner. It is mostly about one person's enthusiasm for a subject being passed on to another. This can also be true of a relationship based on learning a skill such as music, art or carpentry. As long as the intellectual curiosity is mutually shared, no real power imbalance occurs.

You don't have to be discovering a new element or developing a unified field theory to experience intellectual intimacy. This can happen when your interest in any intellectual topic matches with that of another person. Similar interests in philosophy, sociology or political science can provide insights into each other's feelings about life, the universe and everything. It doesn't matter if you are professors of sociology or simply took a continuing education class on the subject. What is important is the open, honest and compassionate discussions which follow.

Spiritual Intimacy

We are not going to define spirituality here because we don't believe there is a single definition. An amazing variety of organized spirituality exists from large organizations to small groups (congregations, covens, monasteries etc.) to single practitioners.

Major organized religious traditions:
(in reverse alphabetical order)

Zoroastrianism, Yazdânism, Wicca, Unitarian Universalism, Taoism, Sikhism, Shinto, Samaritanism, Rastafari, Neo Paganism, Mithraism, Mazdakism, Manichaeism, Mandaeans, Judaism, Jainism, Islam, Hinduism, Gnosticism, Falun Gong, Din-i-Ilahi, Confucianism, Church of All Worlds, Christianity, Buddhism, Bhakti, Bahá'í Faith, Bábism, Ayyavazhi.

This is not an exhaustive list. It does not include tribal religions of Native Americans, African tribes, Australian aborigines or other tribes of any continent.

We are sure the above list is incomplete, but the list covers most population centers around the world. The point is, spirituality is important to people. Asking questions concerning the nature of our existence is cross cultural. Why are we here? Where did it all come from? What does it all mean? How do I fit in? These questions come up for most people.

Many people look to organized religion for answers and for solace during difficult times like loss of work, sickness and death. These gatherings also celebrate and acknowledge good times like a birth, the harvest and marriage. Humans find comfort in gathering together. People have a tendency to gather in community. It is hardly surprising; therefore, that groups based on spirituality should form.

Others meditate, write poetry, practice yoga, or explore altered states of mind with or without the use of drugs. Some come to the conclusion that the questions are unanswerable and that it doesn't matter and just go on about their lives.

People on similar spiritual paths can find comfort and understanding in each other's company. At best it can lead to a deep and loving relationship based on compassion and shared discovery. This can be similar to the intellectual intimacy discussed earlier. We have to acknowledge that there is a lot of "juice" in spirituality because it is so universal. It is not surprising then that people can become involved in a spiritual intimacy.

Touch Intimacy

First thing, we are not talking about sex or sexual foreplay. We are talking about hugs, pats on the back, holding hands, cuddling for comfort; any type of touch which says, I love and support you. People differ widely on how much they want and need of this type of touch. Some people can freely hug someone that they just met. Others are quite selective about the circumstances and from whom they accept touch. Do you remember G.W. Bush giving German Chancellor Angela Merkel an uninvited massage? It was during a G8 summit conference. Talk about inappropriate timing. There were several other reasons this uninvited touch was inappropriate. You can see the Chancellor's reaction to the massage in a video on YouTube. We suggest that you always ask for permission before massaging Chancellors and other strangers.

Touch is something that human beings need. This is particularly true for babies. British psychiatrist John Bowlby did pioneering research that suggests touch from compassionate caregivers allows infants to feel safe and secure. This is the kind of bond a mother has with her baby. Caring touch helps an infant to develop the capacity to create attached relationships later in life. From his initial work Bowlby developed the theory of relationship attachment (Bowlby, 1973).

Part of being a good friend and caring companion is learning a person's needs and wants around touch. You can always ask and if they say "no" don't take it personally. You never know what is going on with the other person. Maybe someone snuck up behind them once and grabbed their shoulders and it still haunts them. It is particularly important to know when touch is not welcome. Unwelcomed touch can seem condescending, intrusive or harassing. If someone is hugging you a little longer than "normal" and you're not bothered by it, stay in the hug. Elon, for instance, shares long "director's cut" hugs with her friends who enjoy them. She is careful not to extend hugs with anyone who is not comfortable with prolonged hugging. If you are uncomfortable in long hugs, it is always your choice to break it. It is important to do what feels best to you.

Financial Intimacy

It's no secret that money is a leading cause of arguments for couples in committed relationships. The internet is full of financial websites that use the term "financial intimacy" in reference to married couples. Their definition is one of open and honest communication while holding respect for each other's needs, wants and desires. Fair enough. We are sure that this definition would work for poly families since most poly folks do their very best to keep open and honest communications between all partners on a variety of topics. Hopefully those communication skills extend to financial matters.

We are going to delve a little deeper into this concept. Married couples have a default deal that when one of the partners die, the other partner gets the marital monies. They don't even have to think about it. (This default can be overridden by the terms of a partner's will or other financial tools that we will discuss in Chapter 5, Finances.) Members of a poly or line family must put into place the proper documentation that says how the real and personal property is distributed. The act of spending the time to make sure those documents exist is another part of our definition of financial intimacy.

Do you and your partners share financial income and expenses? In our family, different partners have had times of prosperity and times of unemployment. The partners who are doing well have always come to the aid of the partner having a tough financial time. All this is done without the expectation of defined repayment. If we were not a financially intimate family, our lives with each other would be quite different. One example, Richard is the handyman of our family. He doesn't charge the family for doing plumbing or electrical repairs to our properties. Yet his work has a cash value. All of this financial melding is done for the good of our family. As a quad we are financially stronger and more stable than any one or two of us would be on our own.

Our financial intimacy was not planned; it evolved as situations came up. Financial intimacy speaks to the concept of the survival of the group benefitting the survival of the individual. It seems like a reflection of the hunter/gatherer tribe mentality that allowed humans, the weakest of the great apes, to survive and thrive for 190-thousand years without the help of agriculture. When we are secure in our basic needs, helping others is generally a part of human nature. When the World Trade Center and Pentagon were attacked on 9-11-2001, Richard immediately went to donate blood. By the time he got to the local blood bank, the line was around the block. When countries are hit by earth quakes, tsunamis and other natural disasters, people from other countries donate money, supplies and volunteers to help those in need.

Creative Intimacy

If you search this term on the web, you are going to be told ways (creative ways) of making your romantic evenings and sex play more fun and different. We're good with sexy costumes, rose petals, incense, reading erotic stories to each other or whatever. That is not what we mean by creative intimacy.

Lists of creative couples are long. In painting and literature alone you find couples such as Willem & Elaine de Kooning; Dorothea Tanning & Max Ernst; Christo & Jeanne-Claude; Mary Shelley & Percy Shelley; F. Scott Fitzgerald & Zelda Sayre; Anaïs Nin & Henry Miller; Simone de Beauvoir & Jean-Paul Sartre; Stephen King & Tabitha King; Samuel Clemens (Mark Twain) & Olivia Clemens. Many of these relationships lasted a long time. Some of the couples collaborate on their art. In other couples, each is an artist in their own right.

Stephen King collaborated with his wife on his first novel, Carrie. In early drafts he felt that his portrayal of the central female character didn't ring true. He threw out the first pages. His wife, Tabitha convinced him to try again and she collaborated by helping him get into the mind of a pubescent teenage girl. Tabitha is not only a supportive wife and collaborator; she is a novelist in her own right. This melding of creative energy is common in the stories of creatively intimate couples.

If you are a creative person (and really, who isn't) how willing are you to let someone into your process. You are laying your ideas bare, open for comment. You make yourself vulnerable opening something as personal as your budding creation to the criticism of another person. You have to trust that this person will give you respectful, constructive comments. Creating art with another person is an act of intimacy.

Recreational Intimacy

Another area where people can relate to each other is recreation. Are you a passionate skier? How about sailing, hiking, miniature golf? There are so many physical activities to choose from. Connecting with another person through a shared interest can be an intimate experience as you help each other to become better at your chosen sport. Many adults think that playing is only for children. Scott G. Eberle, Ph.D, is a strong advocate of adult play and says, "We don't lose the need for novelty and pleasure as we grow up."

While play encompasses a large list of activities, we are focusing on the physical. Some types of play take the form of competition such as badminton or squash. Other forms of play require cooperation and teamwork such as ocean sailing, rock climbing or baseball. Granted, there are solo sailors and even solo rock climbers, adventurous souls who like to work without a net. These sports, and others, can be dangerous. Your safety - even your life - can be in the hands of your partner. We're not saying you must risk your life to develop a recreational intimacy; however, trusting a partner with your safety is a very close bond.

Richard Remembers a Mountain Climbing Partner

"I have been interested in hang gliders from a very young age. Not long after getting out of the Army, I tried my hand at building a hang glider. My climbing partner, whom we shall call Martin, was also interested in the new sport. We took my contraption to a bluff overlooking Puget Sound. A moderate westerly breeze was blowing up the slope, perfect conditions. I picked a spot back from the slope where there was less wind to set up the glider.

Our plan was to first test the glider by flying it like an unmanned kite. We had a decommissioned climbing rope for the test. Our test area was in a Seattle park. A large sandy area was located just back from the bluff's edge. At the edge was a large log with a sign that warned people that climbing down the slope was dangerous. The log looked as if it could have been a telephone pole. We used that log as an anchor for the rope. We harnessed the glider and brought it up into the wind. It took off and flew perfectly. We let the glider fly higher and it took up the slack we had left between the glider and the log. Everything was going fine and we were about to land the glider when the wind picked up. The log started to move. The log was dragged several feet before we could get the glider back on the ground.

Both Martin and I are sailors so that we knew what we were seeing when we looked out over the water. Gust lines were showing on Puget Sound. In the distance we could see white caps forming. Our day of flying was over because the wind was getting too strong. I untied the rope from the glider and had just started to remove the seat harness. Suddenly the glider started to lift from the ground. I thought that I could hold it down by hanging onto the base tube of the control bar. Wrong. As I held onto the glider's control bar, I watched the Earth fall away from my feet. I had no idea about what to do next. The shock of being suddenly yanked into the air was the only thing occupying my mind. Martin yelled, 'Let go!'

A man I trusted with my life gave me a simple and clear instruction. Being preoccupied with hanging onto the glider, I hadn't thought of letting go. But when I heard Martin's voice, I didn't hesitate. I fell several feet into the soft sand and was not hurt. Unfortunately the glider, without a stabilizing weight or rope harness, wasn't so lucky. It crashed and broke all but one of its seven aluminum tubes.

Martin saved my life, or at least saved me from serious injury. Had almost anyone else told me to let go, I would not have responded so quickly. It was my intimate recreational relationship with him that made me trust Martin's instructions without question."

In our research we have discovered definitions for conflict intimacy, work intimacy, parenting intimacy, crisis intimacy, aesthetic intimacy, play intimacy, difficult (hard truth) intimacy and social intimacy. Most of these intimacy definitions are covered, at least in part, by the intimacies we have described here. Mostly we are trying to show you that intimacy comes in many forms and can be shared in many ways.

We have considered some details of eight types of intimacy:

Sexual,

Emotional,

Intellectual,

Spiritual,

Touch,

Financial,

Creative, and

Recreational.

Our guess is that in a stable line family, every member would share at least two of the intimacies from the above list. We're looking for long-term relationship potential and intimacy is one of the strongest reasons for staying together. Imagine a group of 18 to 24 people who all have something in common with you, all of them with matching or complementary interests which keep you motivated. We think that people with whom you connect on multiple levels can be ideal line family partners.

A family such as this does not happen overnight. To develop this sort of arrangement takes time, probably years if not decades. And there is one more profound problem for the first families that attempt this lifestyle – there are precious few role models. As of 2015 we have found a total of 1 actual line family. It is not large, but it has been going for more than 30 years.

To give you an example of the challenge of creating something new, a close friend of ours started out to form a polyamorous family in the early 1970s. She only had science fiction stories as a guide. Some of the men she met gave it a try, but disbelief, jealousy and lack of any support structure made for difficult going. She finally gave up. She was way ahead of her time.

Today poly families are everywhere. Books on the subject abound. Support groups, potlucks, meet-ups and conventions are in most major metropolitan areas around the United States. Polyamory is talked about in the main stream media and has even been included in television series plots and in movies. Most people exploring polyamory have lots of support and role models available.

To be painfully honest, if you are reading this book before the year 2030, there is probably precious little in the way of role models to look to for guidance and support. Except for Robert Heinlein's books, you will not find much about line families… yet. Early adopters always have a tougher time. That is why we are writing this book, to give people a starting point for getting a line family going. As you will discover if you read history and watch the news, the line family model is working for church organizations, corporations, royalty and the richest families in the world. We strongly believe that this will work for polyamorous people.

As to potential line family members, you might be asking, "what about relationships based on a single intimacy from our list, wouldn't they be good enough for a family member"? Indeed they might be. However, we are looking to give a line family relationship the best possible chance for longevity. Let's consider how each single intimacy looks as a standalone basis for an intimate relationship. We break down single-intimacy connections as follows:

Primarily Sexual Relationship

Relationships based primarily on sex fill a human need. In fact Abram Maslow stated in his Hierarchy of Needs (see Chapter 3) that sex is as basic a need as breathing, water, food, sleep, homeostasis and excretion. Maslow does add sexual intimacy in the Love/Belonging level alongside friendship and family. Mutual sexual attraction, which lights up the world, can be amazing for the people involved and that's alright. But sexual infatuation is not a good basis for a long-term relationship. Those relationships that do span years and decades are ones that include other connections. Sex alone only gets you so far. People often refer to chemistry as a cause of the initial attraction. They're right. It is caused by a set of biochemical events in reaction to the new lover. These chemicals can make the new lover seem like the most exciting and attractive person you have ever known… for a while. Beyond that there must be more to sustain the relationship. That's really what we are saying about line family members, that multiple intimate connections will hold the individuals together making for a strong and vibrant family.

Emotional Only Relationship (Perhaps a close or best friend)

What are the qualities of a best friend? People toss that word around, but do we know what we mean? In researching the topic we found a lot of different ideas. But one concept kept coming up, trust. It is great to have someone with whom you can be yourself and trust them not to be too judgmental or to gossip about your quirks. Maybe your best friend is the person you like to hang out with. She or he is a person who sees the world mostly like you do, but with just enough differences to be interesting. Generally close friends are people with whom you laugh. Perhaps you and your best friend share secrets, similar experiences or unconventional ideas. Again trust is a central issue if you do not want your private life made public.

Sounds as if close emotional relationships, or best friends, might be good partners in a line family, but they might not. Best friends are loyal to each other and that loyalty might be a problem in a family. It could happen that the best interest of the family might occasionally be overridden by loyalty to a best friend. We would hesitate to bring best friends into the family at the same time. Perhaps being spread out over time would be better. We have no evidence to back this up, it's just a guess.

Intellectual Only Relationship
(As in a student/mentor relationship)

Mentors in the family could be an excellent relationship. It is a great way to pass along skills such as painting, programming, welding, gardening, auto mechanics, etc. Not only does the student benefit in this relationship, the mentor also gains. Often people learning new subjects ask questions about things that the mentor does not know and must learn for themselves. Also the perspective of a new apprentice can evoke insights for the mentor. It is a poor teacher that learns nothing from their student.

What is the potential for a long-term relationship between a mentor and their protégé or apprentice? If the mentor is capable of eventually accepting their pupil as a colleague rather than a student, the relationship could work out well. The power dynamic must be addressed in the evolution of this type of relationship. Richard has seen this type of relationship work. One of his sisters married one of her professors. That marriage is approaching its 40th anniversary.

Other intellectual relationships can revolve around peers working together on writing projects, fine arts, architecture, inventing… any intellectual skill you can name. These relationships have tremendous potential in and of themselves. Think of Learner and Lowe musicals, Crick and Watson in biology, McCartney and Lennon for rock & roll, Percy and Mary Shelley in literature and Penn & Teller the greatest illusionists and showmen of the day. A line family would do well to nurture these types of collaborations.

You can't expect every collaborative project to be monetarily successful or a cultural achievement. However, the act of working together on a project helps to cement relationships. Sharing the trials and triumphs of even a modest job, such as putting in a few stone stairs on a footpath, gives you a history with your work partner.

Conversely a student/teacher relationship, where the teacher can pass or fail the student, has an imbalance of power. We feel this type of relationship is more temporary and would not be a good basis for a long-term relationship like a line family.

Spiritual Only Relationship

Quite often this is a relationship with a guru or preacher. However, spirituality can also be a relationship between peers, equals on a similar spiritual journey. As stated earlier, spirituality is a common experience among people. We want to know the answers to unanswerable questions and to believe in something. At the root of it all, most would like to believe that there is some purpose to why the Universe exists and that we have a place in it. These questions are normal and can lead to deep and insightful thinking.

Again, if the spiritual relationship is between a spiritual leader and an acolyte, the imbalance of power can lead to loyalties that can override the responsibility that members have to the family. Also a spiritual teacher that is looking for a flock, congregation or other such group can cause its own set of problems in an existing family that is not based on spiritual exploration.

Touch Only Relationship

A relationship based on nonsexual touch alone sounds like a massage therapist and client. Despite how nice it would be to have a professional masseuse in the family, we don't suggest hitting on your massage therapist. If we are talking about a good friend, it is likely the friendship is based on more than touch. People don't allow their personal space to be breached unless you are in a crowded elevator or it is someone with whom you share an interest, hobby, history, etc.

Financial Only Relationship

Financially intimate relationships tend to occur as a matter of course in relationships that have already developed other intimacies. In a line family we think it would be nearly impossible not to have financial relationships with everyone; even if it is based only on your contributions to the family coffers. Other than that, the only financial only relationships we can think of are with a licensed advisor, personal banker or stock broker.

Creative Only Relationship

Creative intimacies can happen where you work. You could find yourself teamed up with another person on consecutive projects because you work so well together and produce excellent results. You might also find this kind of creative relationship in other circumstances such as a writers group, artist circle or any other organized group focused on creative expression. There is also the teacher/student relationship with the same potential for a power imbalance that we described in the section on intellectual relationships.

Recreational Only Relationship

As Richard knows, a recreational intimacy can save your life. But a relationship based solely on recreational interests will ebb and flow with the seasons. You need something else to talk about during the off season of whatever activity you share. Relationships based solely on a recreational activity are generally intermittent at best. Also, people's interest in recreation can change. A partner may be attracted to some new and novel sport that you have no interest in pursuing. Participation in a sport can also be ended by a change in a person's health status.

All of these relationships are good and valuable models for human interaction. However, it bears repeating that we think it takes multiple connections to be a line family member. But that's just our guess.

Before leaving this discussion about intimacy, we want to be clear about one thing – no two relationships are equal. How could they be? What are the metrics for determining if one relationship is equal to another? It has been our experience that every relationship is unique and that relationships vary and evolve over time. This is something to be expected, nurtured and experienced with all of your partners. It is the strength of a line family that all individual members add something different to the whole.

Elon's Opinion on Intimacy

Strong intimate bonds between family members is the glue that will help to keep your family together for generations. Without intimate connections, you will have an intentional community - a lovely thing to have, but not a line family because the members can more easily leave a community. That is why it is important for your family to get to know potential new members well before inviting them to join the family.

CHAPTER TWO

Capital

Open your arms to change,
but don't let go of your values.

Dalai Lama

Types of Capital

Well that's easy. We're talking about money, right? Yes, money is part of what we mean by capital. Having money helps make things happen. Cash, real-estate, stocks, bonds, boats, cars and other personal property and debts make up a person's – or family's – net financial worth. We will talk about all those balance sheet topics in Chapter 5, Finances and Chapter 8, Owning Real Property. But that is only one part of capital. There is also human capital. People can bring value to a line family even if they don't have anything but the shirt on their back.

Have you ever really considered the phrase "making money" or that "people make money"? What do people mean by the phrase, "time is money"? Time is money because the time being counted is human time, not just some period on a clock ticking away its arbitrary units.

With nothing but bare hands, a basket weaver can harvest some free local materials and weave a basket. The basket weaver has just made money if the basket eliminates the need to purchase a similar item. Human knowledge, skill and some free materials have made something of value. The basket's value can be measured by how much money someone is willing to pay or trade for it. The basket also has worth as a tool for the more efficient collection of fruits and vegetables. The basket weaver possesses human capital because of a skill. That is only one type of human capital.

In this chapter we will look at various types of human capital and discover how it could be of value to your line family. Human capital comes under many headings such as biological, intellectual, accomplishment, social and cultural. Some people excel in one or two areas while others have more of a renaissance orientation, a wide range of adequate to excellent abilities.

Biological Capital

We think there are few truer statements than, 'the time you have left is your most valuable possession.' That makes a young person quite wealthy. Young folks usually have physical strength, stamina and a great potential for learning. Young people are a valuable addition to any line family. By young, we mean in their thirties.

Yes, we know it is a generalization, but people in their 20s are really just discovering the world and themselves. Wherever we travel we see young folks hiking, biking and exploring. We are proponents of young people discovering some of the cultural diversity that make up this world. Traveling from a rural upbringing to an urban city lifestyle did wonders for Richard. He found that there were other religions besides Christianity, that people spoke languages other than English and that he never wants to get behind the wheel of a car in England, Australia or anywhere else where people drive on the left side of the road. In short, it gave him a sense of humility and place. He learned there are many ways to see the world and live your life.

As people age, they develop physical skills that range from being fast on a computer keyboard to fine carpentry to martial arts – all physical endeavors that require time to cultivate. Joseph Campbell famously said, "Follow your bliss." He did not mean it as an excuse to just party and have fun. It was more about finding your life's work or purpose. Writing this book is part of following our bliss. It gives our lives a meaning it didn't have a few years ago. It is, we hope, something of us that will last and be of help to people now and in the future. If someone's bliss is architecture and fine carpentry, then they should follow that path. It might not be easy, few worthwhile things are. But it could be rewarding and possibly fun.

Young people who have found their bliss would find a good home in a line family that appreciated, valued or needed the bliss (skills and abilities) he or she has to offer. However, we have found that people's bliss can change. This is because people grow and evolve. We have one friend who started as a dentist. He was good and his patients loved him. He later moved from dentistry to wine making. His talents became widely recognized and he has consulted for dozens of wineries. He is also a gold-medal-winning wine maker. And he can still look in your mouth and give you a pretty good idea of your dental health. So don't expect that young carpenter/architect to stay on that path forever. After all, we are poly people and we like variety.

Intellectual Capital or Knowledge
(Formal and life experience)

Some twenty somethings can spend a lot of time in graduate and postgraduate programs getting advanced degrees. What kind of knowledge could your line family use? How about a medical doctor, lawyer or nuclear physicist? You would be surprised how few times we have been asked if we know a nuclear physicist and could she or he come right over to fix a problem. However their earnings could come in handy and they could be very interesting to converse with.

People in their 40s and beyond not only have formal education, but also have life experience. More practical skills such as electrician, plumber, wine maker, brewer and gardener are just some of the human capital that could be quite valuable. Professional drivers are nice to have around too. There are so many valuable skills that we don't have the time or space to name them all. We have occasionally found out just how expensive professional plumbers are. Diane Christian in her book *Creating A Life Together* puts it succinctly, "realize that your members' skills and energy are equivalent to money." Even better, it's tax free money.

Working for the family also has the benefit of increasing the social glue that holds a family together. When people invest their time, talent and energy in something, they take pride in their accomplishment. The people who benefit from this work grow to appreciate the members who throw themselves into supporting the family. Older family members can also be mentors to younger folks creating more relationships such as described in Chapter 1, Intimacy.

Track Record
(Lifetime accomplishments)

It takes good planning, leadership and determination to see a complex project through. Some people have a natural talent for organizing and inspiring people to work together. Others have studied the skill of management. Let's say your growing line family has someone who has managed several successful Habitat for Humanity projects. A family member with such a proven track record of accomplishment might impress lending officials at a bank to be more inclined to loan your family the money to build that hydroponics, gray water recovery system you've been dreaming about.

If your family includes that wine maker we talked about earlier, you are more likely to get a startup loan for a family winery. If you want to open a bicycle shop, it helps to have a person who has business experience and it doesn't hurt to have a bike mechanic/frame-maker in the family. Loans for a quilting machine for a custom quilt-making business probably will not happen if you don't have at least one experienced quilter in your family.

It's the old saying, nothing succeeds like success. Just thinking that it would be cool to have an ice cream company is not enough if no one in your family has any knowledge of making ice cream or running a business. You will need more than enthusiasm to prove your worth to an investor.

Social Capital
(It's who you know that counts)

Contacts are good to have. Knowing someone at a local bank can help smooth the process of getting a business loan. Knowing people in the city or county planning commission is a help with zoning variances and building permits for that 100 foot, vertical wind turbine/solar power tower you've been dreaming about.

A New Friend of the Community

Sharon is a member of the Cloud Dance Glen intentional community in the Puna district of Hawaii. She shared a story about getting to know people who can help a community. "About 8 years ago we had a renter living in a small structure on the land. He told us that he had little money, but that he had a tent and could build himself a one-room shelter. What he ended up building was not much more than a rickety lean-to that sheltered his tent from the sun. It turned out that all he wanted to do was lie around smoking weed and begging kitchen scraps from us to eat. We finally told him he had to leave. He was not happy with us.

About a week later we received a visit from a planning department inspector. It turns out that our unhappy renter had turned us in for building code violations. Structures built without permits are pretty common in this area. And some of the codes are 'inappropriate' for a tropical jungle climate.

As we talked with the inspector we got the feeling that he didn't really want to bust us. He made comments and suggestions on what he would like to see and not see when he came back to inspect. His recommendations were pretty easy to follow. The next time he visited, we were having a picnic with some of our neighbors. We invited the inspector to hang out, as our inspection was his last appointment for the day. He thanked us, but said that it would look too much like we were paying him off with food for a good inspection report. That's understandable.

Before he left, we handed him some information about our community including a website and a list of community events we had scheduled for the next couple of months. He has attended a couple of potlucks and a movie night. He has become a friend of the community and has helped us out with tips on how to stay on the planning department's good side."

Who do you know in local government? What family members have connections or can make connections? Do you know anyone who works at Adobe™ that will do a little shopping for you at the employees' store? These connections can be cultivated. Volunteer to help political candidates you believe in. When meeting new people the question is often asked, what do you do? Notice where people work. It can be helpful for employment opportunities, discount shopping or meeting people in positions of power. Is this ethical? It all boils down to intent. We would not cultivate a friendship with a person solely based on their ability to economically benefit our family. But if a friendship develops, you will be able to ask for favors if appropriate. It is human nature to want to help other people out.

Even if your line family is off the grid and "self-sufficient" there are always interactions with the outside world. You are connected to the world by taxes, driver's licenses, business licenses, road maintenance, the postal carrier, neighbors, building officials, loan officers and on and on... Knowing people in those worlds makes the inevitable interactions easier.

Cultural Capital
(Religious, racial and economic class)

Speaking of your neighbors – there's your line family just moving onto 25 acres of mixed pasture, orchard and wetland: or you just moved into that grand old inner-city turn-of-the-last-century house with more bedrooms than you can count. Who are your neighbors? What is their culture? You should know; after all you moved into their neighborhood. They will have questions. Unanswered questions turn into speculations that are almost always worse than the facts. Speculations turn into stories based on rumors. Soon your family, according to some neighbors, is a religious cult that will soon have the authorities cordoning off the neighborhood. Seek out your neighbors and talk to them. You don't have to load them up with too much information at first. Just let them know that you are approachable.

Having family members with experience in various cultures helps everyone in the family understand and learn how to treat the people they meet. Your line family will be a challenge to the people in almost any neighborhood you end up in. Sensitivity to people's concerns will help you set their fears to rest or to at least answer questions in their cultural dialect. If you don't know anything about the culture you find yourself in, you will make mistakes. The following story demonstrates the problem of cultural misunderstanding.

A Cultural Dance Around a Desk

Two people lived this story of cross-cultural, miscommunication. The secretary (administrative assistant) was a tall blond woman of Swedish ancestry. The interoffice mail carrier was of Latin American background. One day the secretary had a package that needed special handling. The mail carrier came up to her to receive the package and get the instructions. The secretary retreated from the mail carrier. He moved forward to close the distance. Again the secretary retreated. This cycle repeated several times until the secretary fled into her boss's office and complained that the mail carrier was chasing her around her desk. The mail carrier was investigated for sexual harassment.

What was found to actually be going on was that the secretary's personal space was being violated by the mail carrier. Conversely the mail carrier was trying to establish his personal-space limit that was smaller than the secretary's. No sexual innuendo or threat was intended.

Anthropology teaches us that, in general, cultures near the equator have small personal space requirements. The farther north you go, the greater the personal space becomes (in the cultures of Europe anyway). In addition, people from rural settings have larger personal space requirements than folks who have lived in urban areas for a generation or more. In the above case, the secretary thought she was being sexually harassed while the mail carrier thought she was being rude.

So let's say you are a person of Italian descent who has lived in the city all your life. You and your line family have found your perfect urban acreage and are about to meet your neighbors of Irish lineage who are life-long farmers. You approach the father of the family with a smile on your face, hand held out as he quickly stumbles over himself moving backwards from your attack. Not a good first meeting. If only you had someone in your family who knew about the personal space difference, they could have warned you not to move too close.

Cultural signals are little land mines everywhere we turn, just waiting to blow up a potential friendship. If you have no one in your family familiar with the type of neighborhood to which you are moving, find a friend or guide to help with these initial contacts. It is a tried and true saying that you don't get a second chance to make a first impression. And a good working relationship with your neighbors is a type of capital itself.

We end this chapter with an unfinished story from one of the communities we visited doing research for this book. We don't know how it will resolve, but there are some lessons to be learned.

Changing Social Environments and Zoning

When Richard first visited Hawaii in the early 80s, he was amazed at how many multi-story buildings (such as the hotel where he had stayed in Kona) had no exterior walls on the ground floor. When we went to the big island in January of 2015 to do research for this book, we took a side trip to Kona, the dry side of the island. Richard was surprised to see that the open-air architecture he loved in the 80s was gone, except for a few restaurants. It was due to changes in the building codes. It has affected some of the communities we visited.

Moonrise Glenn Collective formed in the mid-80s. The founders bought land that was remote – even by Puna District standards. As the years went by, the area next to Moonrise Glenn started to be developed.

It took many years for the neighborhood to become fairly populated. The homes that went in were mostly for upper middle class retired people or younger IT professionals who had retired in their 30s and 40s. For a number of years the residents of Moonrise Glenn invited their neighbors to a monthly potluck. As the neighborhood became more populated, the potluck got bigger and bigger. The neighbors who had moved in started inviting their friends. As the potluck grew, it seemed that fewer and fewer people knew that "potluck" meant that you showed up with food to contribute to the party. When neighborhood children started showing up without their parents to eat, the community decided that the potluck needed to end.

Other community events continued however. The weekly community market was a source of money for the residents. They would sell produce, arts and crafts. They also rented booth space to other folks to sell products. Additional income came from renting space for weddings and other special events. Moonrise Glenn also used to produce an annual variety show with proceeds split between the community and a charitable cause.

Moonrise Glenn is going through lots of changes due to issues with the county and state of Hawaii. This was mostly caused by a few neighbors who have moved in next to the community. They complain that they want to be in a "normal" upper-middle class subdivision. A sustainable intentional community on their periphery is not in their vision of what a "normal" subdivision should be. Richard blames their real estate agents and brokers who should have disclosed information about the established community living next to the subdivision.

Neighbors have filed complaints with the County of Hawaii against the community for noise and zoning violations. Inspectors from the county have charged the community with various violations. Some of the most common violations are for building code issues. For example, the common kitchen/dinning building is a sturdy structure with an excellent roof. A good roof is important in a jungle with over 100 inches of rain a year.

A space such as this has some special requirements. Because the kitchen produces heat and a lot of water vapor, there must be excellent ventilation. This community (like many others) has opted for using screens for the majority of the exterior walls. This not only provides ventilation, it also lets in natural light and allows for passive cooling of the space. It also keeps insects from getting into the building.

Unfortunately the building code requires solid walls and windows to be used on the building exterior. This type of construction requires the addition of mechanical ventilation fans and air conditioning. The resulting larger energy requirements would increase the community's utility bills or necessitate installing more solar panels and support equipment.

The basic lesson we take from the developing situation at Moonrise Glenn is to either look "normal" or be remote from judgmental neighbors.

Elon's Opinion on Capital

Wouldn't it be great if you could decide what careers and skills you would like for your line family members to have and then just go "pick them off the poly tree"? There are plenty of New Age gurus teaching about Abundance and saying that it is exactly what you should do - create your list and the universe will bring the people to you. It sounds great! I have found that I more often get what I want if I know what it is that I want. So go ahead and make your list, and keep it in mind as you meet "persons of interest". I hope that you will also be open to "loving the one you are with", too. They may not be exactly what you were looking for but may turn out to be exactly what your line family needs - now and/or in the future.

CHAPTER THREE

Vision and Agreements

The best way to predict the future is to design it.

R. Buckminster Fuller

If you want to go fast, go alone.
If you want to go far, go together.

An African proverb

Without change there can be no life.
With unceasing change there can be no peace.

Elon de Arcana

What holds a group of people together; love, loyalty, tradition, community, a wall, a border? Gravity seems to be the only thing holding the human race together sometimes. The question of what holds people together in community and family is one of the most important questions facing a polyamorous line family.

In 1943 Abram Maslow published a paper titled, "A Theory of Human Motivation." In it he described a hierarchy of needs. He ordered them from basic survival needs to higher orders of human fulfillment. The 5 levels of his hierarchy are, from lowest to highest: Physiological, Safety, Love/Belonging, Esteem and Self-Actualization.

Self – Actualization:
morality, creativity, spontaneity, problem solving, lack of prejudice, acceptance of facts.

Esteem:
self-esteem, confidence, achievement, respect for others, respect by others.

Love/Belonging:
friendship, family, sexual intimacy.

Safety:
security of: body, employment, resources, morality, the family, health, property.

Physiological:
breathing, water, food, sleep, sex, homeostasis, excretion

A. Maslow, 1943

What we find interesting is that family is mentioned twice in Maslow's levels of human needs. Family is found in both Safety and Love/Belonging. Maslow believed that a family provides safety to the individual members. This occurs because in a family you are surrounded by people whom you care about and who care about you. That is especially true for a "family of choice". It supports our contention that line families are a way to stay safe in a world of economic and political upheavals. Family also provides a support mechanism during times of personal emotional trials.

A Question of Meaning and Purpose

Before going into the details of family vision statements and agreements, we will address a fundamental question; what is the difference between a line family and an intentional community? We have been asked that question at nearly every presentation we've given. Until we started interviewing intentional communities for this book, we mostly gave somewhat vague answers. We talk about commitment to the family vs. commitment to a community. We mention the different intensities of relationships between a life-long friend and an acquaintance at work. The following story, however, brought the difference between a line family and intentional community into sharp focus.

Why George Might Leave

Please don't misread our intentions in telling this story. We very much admire and respect the communities that this story is based on. We mean no disrespect and we sympathize with the situations in which these communities find themselves.

Hawaii is the home of the Bent Branch Collective. As with the other Hawaiian communities we visited, they are located in the Puna district. Until recently they had 13 full members. Rosie tells us what happened. "About 9 months ago we had a work party repairing and upgrading our barn. We were putting in a new roof and repairing the siding. Our oldest member, George, was working on the ground cutting and stacking materials needed for the job. While carrying a bundle of siding planks George tripped and fell. He injured his back.

His back had been giving him trouble for some time. That is why he was not working on the roof or on a ladder. We didn't know how serious the injury might be. George was helped to his home. He felt that all he needed was a couple of days of bed rest. During that time various members of the community helped him by bringing him food, washing his laundry and helping with bathroom chores. None of us have any real medical training beyond some basic first aid, but I think we did a pretty good job.

After 18 days George was not feeling any better. He decided to go to the hospital. He was there for several days. He was found to have a ruptured disc and pinched nerve. He now wears a back brace and takes regular pain medications. When he returned George could take care of himself, but he wasn't supposed to do any real physical labor, even sweeping the floor was not recommended. He helps a little in the kitchen, but lifting or carrying anything is right out."

Rosie sighed and the rest of the community members were silent. After a moment we asked what their plans might be if George didn't get any better? Elroy asked Rosie if he could answer that. Rosie nodded. Elroy explained that they had not really planned for this situation. "When we started the community just over 25 years ago, getting old wasn't in our plans."

The other community members muttered and nodded their agreement. Elroy continued, "We were focused on the present. Not really considering things that would happen way off in the future. As it stands today, we have no plans for taking care of older or disabled community members. We are too small and too poor to deal with aging people." Elroy grew silent.

Judy volunteered an idea being considered. "We can do a couple of things. We can adopt a change in George's monthly dues to reflect the added cost of his care and upkeep. The problem is that I don't think George has the money to manage that. Otherwise we will have to explore with George how to co-create an exit strategy. It's like Elroy said, we are poor, or what I really should say is that we don't have much in the way of savings. We can't afford to provide or pay for a member's long-term personal care requirements."

Jane, the community secretary added a final observation. "I don't think that any of us planned on living out our lives here. But as a group, the majority of us are older than 50. It would be too much for us to expect a few younger people to support and care for us."

As we said at the beginning of this story, we totally get what is happening at the Bent Branch Collective. Also, we don't want to say that all intentional communities are unprepared for caring for their older or disabled members.

One great example of an intentional community being prepared for ageing members is Twin Oaks. But Twin Oaks has two things going for it that Bent Branch lacks. First is a larger adult population with a good range of ages. Twin Oaks generally has around 100 members. Their second advantage is having several successful community businesses. As a community, Twin Oaks makes good money and has learned how to manage it over the years. In consideration for their elder members, the requested weekly work hours are reduced by one hour for every year over the age of 50. In addition, refurbished electric golf carts are available for people with mobility issues.

Bent Branch and Twin Oaks are two extremes on the issue of disabled and ageing community members. The reason we bring this up is that our vision of a line family includes members living out their lives with the support of a financially strong family of loving people willing to share in caring for the elderly members of the family.

Family Vision Statement

Merriam Webster defines the type of vision we are talking about as "A thought, concept, or object formed by the imagination." Therefore a vision statement is a document of beliefs, broad long-term goals and values that are shared by the line family members.

A shared vision is a must for a cohesive group of investors, explorers, parishioners… and members of a line family. If you have people who enjoy urban living and want to stay close to cultural activities, they will be unlikely candidates for the rural eco-farming family that wants to grow all their own food and home-school the children. A vision is what people get passionate about; it is what people will use to keep themselves inspired. When people ask you what your family is all about, you can describe your core values because you have taken the time to write them down, rewrite them and revise them until they fit comfortably.

A vision statement is better when it is not a rigid document. A vision statement that is available for comment, review and modification makes it - and your family - resilient and adaptable to change. Remember, the world changes - everything changes. Let your vision statement be a living document. For example, in 1967 the original founders of the intentional community Twin Oaks had a vision that all meals would be communal. The idea was to foster a community awareness and self-identity for the group. As time went on, some people wanted to share some meals with a few select members of the community. The community agreements were revised (after much discussion) and "affinity groups" were allowed to form. Twin Oaks discovered that relationships are not equal and some are more intense than others.

A fine line exists between having a vision that is too broad and one that is too narrowly defined. Say your family's overall vision is that of an artist's collective. Would you define painting as an art? For some painting is a craft. They understand the rule of thirds, stress and balance and how to use a color wheel. They use these skills to produce mass market "art" for craft fairs and motel rooms. We have seen fine examples of this and celebrate their financial success. It might be that they are doing this to support their "serious art," the work that is important to them and that they are passionate about.

What about jewelry making, or is that a craft as well? Are crafters what you want in your vision or only what you consider to be "true" artists? Is a crafter's work likely to generate more income for your family? Will you require all the artists in your family to produce work for sale? Do you want to restrict the number of artists working in a particular medium or do you want a family of primarily painters? Don't ask us, this is your choice to make with the initial partners in your family. Just remember, if your vision is too closely drawn and narrowly focused, you may not get new members and your line family might not survive for more than one generation.

What about a too broadly drawn vision? Do you see your family populated with college and university graduates? If so, how well would the hard science folks get along with the theology majors? It could be fun, it could be a disaster, we are not sure as we have no real experience with that. It might be great having that broad range of thought involved closely with each other. Finding a vision that inspires a variety of individuals to join your family – people who will all get along – will be difficult. Don't worry; there are "do overs" in this endeavor. If you are forming a line family in the first half of the 21st century, you are pioneers. Don't expect things to be easy.

A vision statement encompasses large ideas. One of the biggest is where to live in terms of urban, suburban or rural environments. This should be in the vision statement with supporting ideas as to why a particular social setting is best for your family. Another topic you might consider for your vision statement is defining the common values your family holds. The following list contains suggestions to get the conversation started. Pick and choose what seems right, add other ideas not listed and disregard the rest.

Adventure	*Birthrate*	*Charity*	*Children*	*Civility*
Communication	*Creativity*	*Egalitarianism*	*Education*	*Elderly*
Environment	*Exploration*	*Faith*	*Freedom*	*Fun*

Health	*Humor*	*Integrity*	*Kindness*	*Knowledge*
Love	*Openness*	*Security*	*Service*	*Sharing*
Spirituality	*Tolerance*	*Transparency*	*Wisdom*	

In our interview with the Moonrise Glenn intentional community, the subject of fun as part of their shared vision came up. Tina, one of the members, told us, "You should enjoy each other's company and have fun together. Laughing is part of the glue that holds a family together."

We asked her if she had any examples of fun activities that the community shared? Tina described a game they invented. "It is played with a piece of paper. The first person draws a small picture at the top of the page and hands it to second person. The second person is the only person who should see the picture. They write a sentence just below the picture. It's the start of the story. The paper is then folded so that the next person only sees the sentence. That person draws a small picture inspired by the sentence and folds the paper so that only the new picture is showing. We keep passing the paper around until it is full. If we feel the need, we can continue this on a second page, but usually we just stop when the page is full. Then the paper is unfolded and the whole story is read. The stories get really bizarre, especially when a drawing was not very good and was interpreted entirely differently from what the artist intended."

Another game the family plays is spoons. If you look online you will find a lot of different versions of the game. Some like to play in an orderly manner with a full deck of cards or even two decks. Moonrise Glen likes a faster more chaotic game. Bob explains the rules.

"You always have a shortage of spoons in the game. You use one less spoon than the number of players. Like with 5 players, there are 4 spoons on the table. With five players we collect all the aces, ones, twos, threes, fours and fives out of a deck and use them to play. The cards are shuffled and all the players get four cards. You can never have more than four cards in your hand. You discard one of your cards to the person on your left and pick up the card discarded by the person on your right. Everyone does this at the same time, none of this taking turns stuff. When someone gets four of a kind they grab a spoon from the table. Then everyone grabs for a spoon. The person who didn't get a spoon writes an 'S' on their score pad. The game is repeated until someone has spelled the word 'SPOON' on their score card."

Linda, who had been very quiet during our interview, was suddenly excited. "Tell them about the hidden spoon version." Bob looked at Linda and asked her to explain it to us.

"Ok, well we thought it would be fun if getting a spoon off the table was more of a challenge. Sometimes we will put spoons into empty tin cans, shoe boxes, empty cereal boxes – anything big enough to hold a spoon that you can't see into. There are more boxes and cans than there are spoons. So when the first person with four of a kind starts looking for a spoon, everyone can start looking for spoons. It means that the first person with four of a kind might not even get a spoon."

"There is really no strategy involved," Bob added. "The children have an equal chance of winning. The kids love the game and it's very humbling for smart people."

We feel it is important for a family to have fun together. The spoons game is a true all-ages activity. If you want to explore the importance of play for people of all ages, we recommend starting with the following TED talk:

http://www.ted.com/talks/stuart_brown_says_play_is_more_than_fun_it_s_vital?language=en

You can find this link on the book's companion website www.line-family.info/CALF_companion/.

Creating your family vision statement should be a shared project that includes input from all family members. All line families will be different.

There is no one family vision that is correct and superior to all others. Your family vision is not likely to be the same in three or four generations. But having a good vision to start with gives a solid foundation for future generations when they need to adapt to different social and political realities.

Be prepared to spend time creating your vision statement. It may be short in length, but its meaning to your family is big. Revisit it often. Having a clearly defined vision for the family provides one of the social glues that help to create strong relationship bonds and long-term stability for a line family. A vision statement can also provide the family with a sense of meaning and purpose. It lets line family members know that they are a part of something that is bigger than themselves. If the vision statement needs to be modified, look in Chapter 7, Family Decision Making for techniques and methods of deciding how to revise this important document.

Elon and one of our other family members were once involved in a group that had been going along merrily, meeting once a month for about year. Then the leaders of the group decided that the group should have a vision statement. The group spent several months debating it, and then eventually broke up because people got bored with the process, and disenchanted because the members could not discover a common vision. That may sound like a good reason to avoid creating a vision statement. However, if the group had started out with a vision statement already in place it might still be going strong.

Family Agreements

Your vision statement describes generally agreed to values; it probably has no legal standing. A family agreement however, can be the basis of an LLC's operating agreement. For more details, see Chapter 11, Cohabitation Arrangements. A family agreement covers specific issues and practical topics that come up in the day-to-day workings of a line family. Where a vision statement is usually fairly brief and defines broad concepts, family agreements get into the details of how the vision might be achieved. Many of life's daily details are worked out in a family agreement. For example, must everyone live on the same property and/or under the same roof? That is an issue best dealt with in the family agreement. We know of poly families that have some members who are seasonal residents due to work or weather considerations. Your family might have several properties, or perhaps being sequestered on a family compound is what you're about. Get this clear in your family agreement and be prepared to modify it as your family's situation changes and grows.

A Story of Evolution and Change

Radiant Springs intentional community was founded in the early 80s by a group of self-described anarchists. They actually called it a commune for the first few years (see Chapter 10, Random Notes). These community founders were in their mid- to late 20s and early 30s.

It was an idealistic group. They looked at the world and didn't like what they saw. They talked about the pollution of the ground, air and water. They despaired at the continuing loss of rainforests and species extinctions. Because things looked so bad, they decided – as a community – that they would not bring children into the world. It was their first true consensus decision – even though none of them knew about the process of consensus. Most of the founders were still at Radiant Springs 10 years later. Also, most of them were married and had at least one child.

Other overturned decisions were revealed as some of the members of Radiant Springs talked about their past. One issue is wild chickens. They are a bit of a problem, especially the roosters. Meg has a real issue with roosters. She told us, "Some people don't mind because they are strong sleepers and they do not hear the crowing, but I'm a light sleeper who gets woken up by mosquito farts. These roosters start crowing at three in the morning." Wild rooster hunts have limited but not eliminated the problem.

"Now Brian has a pet rooster," Meg complained. "I am not sure what that's about. At least he is about as far away from my jungalow as possible. I wear earplugs when I sleep. It helps."

Another community decision was that there would be no dogs on the property. But as with babies and roosters, one of the community members showed up with a dog one day. Glen had been raised on a farm and grew up with dogs. After two years in the community, he finally gave in to his desire to have a dog.

Lois raised her head from her hands, "It's hard to say no to anything because someone will want what you said no to. What the community does is try to come to some agreement about the restrictions around whatever the situation is. The real issue for me is people deciding on their own to go against community decisions."

We discovered that these "community decisions" were not incorporated into the bylaws. Meg thought that the rule against roosters had been written down. Lois admitted that these community policies were rarely written down, "and even if they are, our record keeping is not that great."

We are not sure whether this lax recording and enforcing of community decisions is one of the reasons this community has survived for 25 years or not. We don't think that we got the full story. We also don't think that any of the "rule violations" were malicious. In Radiant Springs' evolution, the members seem to have accepted that their initial view of how life should work was, perhaps, a little naïve and restrictive. The ability to change and grow seems to be an important concept in successful intentional communities. Peter wrapped up a basic community concept, "We allow for everyone to be who they are."

What are your family agreements about communal meals, property maintenance, parenting, household work and expenses? Your family must also decide what issues need to be left out of your agreement. There is a lot you need to look at. Just be prepared to take a long time in writing the 1st draft of your family agreements. What's a long time? A year at least, maybe two; after all, you are building a multigenerational family. What's two years for an important document that will live and evolve for generations?

Note: You can use an initial, somewhat brief, draft of your family agreements as the operating agreement of a family LLC. Just make sure that you include language that allows your family to modify the operating agreement.

Combining Work and Play

Here is a story that explores the relationship between work and fun. Cloud Dance Glen is an intentional community on the big island of Hawaii. The original 6 members purchased the land in 2002 as joint tenants. The land was converted to a land trust in 2009 after the communal structures were built.

A pond had been installed by the previous owner. Volcanic rock doesn't hold water very well. That is why there are only two natural lakes on the island. The main problem with the pond was that it was built at the lowest point on the property. That meant it couldn't be used for irrigation or any other type of passive water distribution system. The other problem with the pond was that you couldn't see it. Jungle plants had totally covered the pond.

If it couldn't be used for anything else, people wanted to be able to at least see the pond. Eric devised a plan. "I believe in making work fun whenever possible so I proposed a plant pulling party. Everybody agreed. On the appointed day we loaded a cooler with ice, bottles of water, soda and a couple of beers. We hauled it out to the pond. Everybody took off all their clothes. We don't wear that much clothing here, so the pile was pretty small. And we all waded in and started tugging on the plants. I'm not quite sure how it started, but somebody lost their balance when a vine came loose. The wet plant went flying and hit Sheila in the back. She let out a shriek and turned while throwing the leaves she had in her hand towards the person flailing in the water. Of course they didn't fly straight and hit both Sharon and Stan. Things just sort of escalated from there.

Soon everyone was soaked and covered in vegetable matter. I think Kenny was the first to walk out of the pond and shake the plants off onto the pile of vegetation we had been pulling. He waded back into the pond and was immediately covered with plants again. Soon everyone was traipsing up to the pile and shedding their plants and returning to the fray. I'm not sure how long this lasted, but by the time we all collapsed on the ground exhausted and laughing, we had cleared about a quarter of the pond. It took the jungle about two or three days to repopulate the area we had cleared. We figured the jungle had won that round. But it was a fun fight."

Don't forget to come to an agreement about the optimal number of adult members you want in your family. Our own opinion is that an optimal number lies somewhere between 12 and 24. Don't take this as a rule, it is one of our guesses. As the culture changes the optimal number might get bigger. We envision a time when clusters of line families live next to, or at least near each other. A cluster of line families would be an amazing intentional community.

Parenting issues should be discussed, preferably before children are brought into the family. Remember that your line family does not require children to continue through the generations. But let's be practical, babies do happen. Also your family might look at the possibility of adoption. Under "normal" circumstances adoption can be difficult. We have no idea how a line family might look to an adoption agency. If you already have children and lots of resources, it might be possible. And as culture changes, line families might become the preferred adoptive situation; but we are getting ahead of ourselves here.

As a personal note, you do not need to be genetically related to a child to share in the joys and heartache of child rearing. You only need to be open to an emotional connection. It is our experience that children know when someone loves and cares for them. Children totally get the "emotionally poly" concept.

How will maintenance and upkeep of family property be handled? We are talking about things beyond the daily issues of dishes and laundry. House painting, remodeling, vehicle maintenance and other major repair issues have a way of coming up at the worst possible times. Do you have family members with experience in plumbing? If so you are lucky, plumbing is expensive to hire out. However, you should not take advantage of your family member's expertise without some kind of compensation and acknowledgement. How will your family do that? You might reduce or eliminate their monthly financial contribution to the family bank account for an agreed upon period of time. Most people appreciate being acknowledged for their special efforts and contributions. No matter what kind of family or community you find yourself in, it is important that you don't take people for granted.

This brings us to a major issue in family agreements, money to support the line family. How much money and/or in-kind work is expected from each member to support the line family? It is our opinion that a family bank account should grow over the years so that the family members – individually and collectively – can survive hardships and take advantage of opportunities. In Chapter 5, Finances we talk about creating reserve accounts for costs such as regular maintenance, emergency repairs, family vacations, parties, etc. as a way of establishing a family budget. It is an excellent topic for your family agreements.

Just to be clear: we believe that all members of the family should have their own personal money and possessions. This allows for personal expression and freedom of action. We are not advocates of communal systems that eschew all personal property ownership. People are individuals with different needs and wants even in the most perfectly balanced line family. That is why we started this chapter with Maslow's 5 levels of self-actualization. Traits that make us individuals are in the two highest levels of Maslow's hierarchy.

At Twin Oaks there is a requirement of 42 hours of work per week to support the community. Lots of things that people might not consider work are included in a community member's weekly work total. These can include tending the garden as well as making music and performing for the community's entertainment. At the other extreme is the Windward Line Family. They have a minimum requirement of 2 hours a day, 6 days a week. Amazing things get done at Windward despite their modest work requirement in part because the majority of people contribute more than 2 hours a day by choice.

Will your line family develop businesses? If so, what kinds of guidelines will the businesses adhere to so that they reflect your family's values? You might want all your businesses to use locally sourced raw materials whenever possible. Perhaps your businesses could strive to use renewable sources of energy. Maybe your businesses should be union shops. All of these ideas, and more, are good topics for discussion when considering a family business venture.

Note: You probably should not include the topic of dating in any legal documents. It might make that document null and void. More details are found in Chapter 11, Cohabitation Arrangements. However, that doesn't mean that a family agreement about dating can't be written down in a separate document. We think it should be written out so that people can refer to it when the need arises.

Dating protocol is a basic issue that needs to be established early. For any open poly family the question of safer sex practices is an important issue. As the size of your family grows, the issue becomes even more important.

Beyond just dating is the issue of when a person becomes a prospective family member. At some point the potential member has to start interacting with the rest of the family. Everyone must know and be relatively comfortable with possible new members. This will take more and more time as the family grows. Hopefully this person will develop working relationships and friendships with the other family members. Some of these friendships could become sexual. Before the person is asked to join your family should additional sexual relationships be encouraged or discouraged?

Our guess is that a potential member could start getting involved in family projects, businesses or events that let everyone have a chance for interactions with the new person. This would take up a lot of the potential member's time. From a practical standpoint, the more members your line family has, the more time it will take for everyone to get a sense of how this new person might fit into the family. Richard likes the idea of taking a year and a day to get to know a potential family member. But that's just one opinion. Whatever you decide should probably be in the non-public portion of the family agreements. If their growing involvement with the family takes them away from their regular employment, should that person be supported financially for some period? Should they live with the family? How much time does the potential member need to spend with the family as opposed to the personal time spent with the member who initiated the relationship? There is New Relationship Energy (NRE) to deal with. The disruptive nature of NRE might be easier for a large line family to deal with. A triad or quad that has a family member spending a lot of time with a new love can be disruptive to the daily life of the family. This is new territory. As yet there are no established role models, that we know of, for adding partners to a line family of 12 or more people.

One common feature we have noticed in long-term relationships, whether they be monogamous or poly, is that each member of the relationship has a private space. This has generally taken the form of a separate room. For those of you into the tiny house revolution, try letting everyone have a separate desk. While that might seem pretty minimal this has actually worked well for us when we occupied a 200 square foot living space while writing this book. Occasionally we have seen the private space requirement go so far as separate residences.

Amelia Earhart is the most famous person we have found, so far, who clearly stated a need for privacy from her husband. It is in her prenuptial agreement that, "… I may have to keep some place where I can go to be myself, now and then, for I cannot guarantee to endure at all times the confinement of even an attractive cage." We agree that personal space is a human need that is sometimes at odds with the human need for companionship and touch. This must be considered by any line family when making housing plans.

While on the subject of Amelia Earhart's prenup it is also interesting to note that she included language about non-monogamy. She did not want either her husband or herself to be bound by "any midaevil [sic] code of faithfulness." The entire document can be found at, www.purdue.edu/uns/images/earhart.newdocs/earhart.prenup.jpeg.

A Brief Introduction to Family Investing

An important issue is your family's investment strategy. As time goes on, this strategy should probably change as the family portfolio grows. Your best course is to study the subject of investing. There are many books, college classes and websites available to give you an idea about the large array of investment opportunities available. When you have some knowledge about investing you might employ the services of a licensed investment counselor. There are more details in Chapter 5, Finances.

How will your family make choices about where to invest money, what business ventures to start and who to add to the family? Big questions. Fortunately we have whole chapters dedicated to these subjects. In particular this chapter and the chapters on Finances, Owning

Real Estate, and Family Decision Making will cover these discussions and be a starting point for developing your own ideas.

Unexpected expenses happen to all individuals and families. Cash on hand is almost always a good thing. It is helpful to have contingency plans in place for the unexpected such as power outages, severe storms and other natural and manmade calamities. Tools should be in your family agreement. What major communal tools does your household require? We are not talking about screwdrivers or wrenches. We mean expensive tools such as welding equipment, lathes, drill presses, 16-foot long-arm quilting machines - that is big ticket items. Weapons - what kind will you allow and for what purposes? The answers to these questions for a rural family will probably be different from the answers for an urban professional family. Emergency preparedness kits will also vary widely. If you live on a farm with a stocked root cellar, other emergency food supplies will not be as important for you as it will be for the urban family.

Your family agreement is likely to be a large document. It will grow and evolve over the years – and it should. We recommend that your family schedule a regular, formal review of the family agreement document. Keep the family agreements fresh and relevant to whatever situation your family finds itself in. Other topics you might include in your family agreement could be: how interpersonal disputes are handled, what kind of parenting system do you want, how to handle family of origin issues, what traditions, rituals and events you want to create for the family, etc. Again, this list is just a conversation starter. It is not a set of instructions for what your line family should be doing.

Elon's Opinion on Vision and Agreements

Richard and I spoke to members of several intentional communities while we were writing this book. One of the things that people mentioned time and time again was the importance of having a common vision. They told us of communities they knew of that did not last very long. The people we talked with felt that the lack of common interests and goals kept the other people from really coming together as a group. When times got tough, people simply left. A well stated group vision will help to attract new members who are in alignment with your family's vision, and the intimate connections that we talked about in Chapter 1, Intimacies will contribute to moving that vision forward.

One type of agreement that we only briefly mentioned in this chapter is agreements around sexual behavior, within the family and with people outside of the family. There can be a lot of jealousy that is stirred up by sexual relationships, not to mention the issue of STDs. Having well thought out agreements about when, where, with whom, and under what circumstances sex will be happening will save trouble later. Even if the agreement is "anything goes", it is important that all members are aware of and comfortable with that decision. If the agreement is restrictive in any way, but not actually set down on paper, hearing "oh, I didn't know about that" after a sexual encounter happens can cause unnecessary problems. So be clear and revisit the agreements on a regular basis (annually?) to see if they are still the agreements that the family is comfortable with, and that all family members are following the agreements. If it is found out that one or more of the family agreements, sexual or otherwise, are not being followed, you may hear someone say, as our family members hate to hear each other say, "we need to talk!" In that case, the information in Chapter 7, Family Decision Making may come in handy.

CHAPTER FOUR

Household Management

We are called to be the architects of the future, not its victims.

Joel Garreau

Whether your family has a 50-room mansion, several linked row houses or several large homes in scattered locations there are practical matters that all home owners must address. These matters can be more (or less) complicated in a large multi-adult household.

We have interviewed a number of polyamorous families that have been together for more than 3 years. Why 3 years? Because Dan Savage, editor of the Stranger and author of the weekly column Savage Love, said that while he had been to a few poly commitment ceremonies, he had never been to a poly family 3rd anniversary party. To be fair, he admitted that it was "an asshole thing to say." Richard wrote to him and politely told him about our family that, at the time, was approaching its tenth year. This resulted in a phone conversation with Dan and his learning about long-term poly families. Our interviewees had been in their poly households for 3 to 13 years when we spoke to them. It is not a large sample by scientific standards, but it is a starting point for ideas on how to run a multi-adult household.

We interviewed 2 triads composed of 2 men and 1 woman, 2 triads with 2 women and 1 man and a quad family with 2 women and 2 men. We also interviewed a few residents of a local cohousing group.

Household Chores

Several techniques surfaced for splitting tasks such as washing dishes, laundry, vacuuming, lawn care, gardening and so on. One family claimed to have no set plan saying, "Things just get done." In closer questioning we learned that when a chore is accomplished, the person lets the family know and that person is acknowledged and thanked. Each individual seemed to have a mindset that no one should have to do the same chore more than 2 times in a row. Other partners would make an effort to take care of that chore the next time it came up "leapfrogging" the person who had last worked on the task.

Leapfrogging did not happen when a party was scheduled, everyone put in effort wherever it was needed. This family has a large house and can entertain a lot of guests. The family likes to host parties and entertain. When preparing for a party they are all in on the fun - cooking, cleaning, moving furniture, setting up and cleaning and breaking it all down afterwards. What we call "leapfrogging" only happened in this one family in our sample.

We used to doubt a line family of 12 or more could work the leapfrogging concept to everyone's satisfaction. However, on a trip to a co-housing community we observed that much the same type of concept was being used to run the communal kitchen. They have a magnetic scheduling board. Everyone has their name printed on tiny rectangular magnets (similar to magnetic poetry word magnets found on many refrigerators). Kitchen and dining room shifts can be selected up to two weeks in advance. To be fair we must mention that this group has only 5 communal meals a week. With over 2-dozen adult members, this is not too onerous a schedule. When an individual or individuals use the kitchen, they clean up after themselves.

Everyone else had some kind of schedule. All the schedules were modified in some way. For instance if one person did not have a regular 8-hour/day job, that person took on more – but not all – of the household responsibilities. In one family the man loved to cook and was good at it. Therefore he did most of the cooking and less of the dish washing. The overall theme seemed to be flexibility, a willingness to adjust the schedule as issues came up such as hosting parties, going on dates, separate vacations, etc. A common comment was that everyone could speak up if they felt they were being treated unfairly. In the family that had no schedule, it seemed as if household chores were often done by two or more of the family members together. We can see why a schedule might not work for them. A schedule might tend to isolate these family members. Once everyone's names are in the schedule boxes, it might start to alter their behavior. If you are scheduled to do a task by yourself, you might not want to pitch in on other nights. As long as this family is happy and things get done, why change it? Maybe this schedule-free style of household management would work for your family, maybe not.

Most other families used a variety of calendar scheduling. Our favorite is the rotating chore wheel that varies the days that each person does a chore. That way no one person is assigned to clean up the kitchen every Saturday night. If you have a lot of weekend parties and events at your house, the Saturday person might be overly burdened. On the other hand, the Saturday night person might always have lots of help and have the easiest day in the schedule. The search for egalitarian solutions is not always easy.

Speaking of difficult searches for egalitarian solutions, what about sleeping arrangements? The Kerista Commune of San Francisco (1971 – 1991) had a rotating sleep schedule so that everyone had a different partner every night. Was that an egalitarian solution? Maybe, but we believe strongly in everyone's right to be at choice when it comes to any type of intimate connections. None of the families we interviewed had any type of set schedule except for one MFM triad. In this family one of the male partners sleeps alone most nights due to his snoring issues. We suggest that sleeping arrangements and personal space issues should be fully discussed and that some general initial agreements be made with new members of your line family. More detail can be found in Chapter 3, Family Vision and Agreements. Remember that we don't expect every relationship in a line family to include sexual intimacy.

Family Expenses

Utilities, food, maintenance, travel, cable TV and Internet all cost money. How much does each family member pay? Some methods used to cover costs include percentages based on income, equal division or based on the use of the service or product. In one family there was an individual that had little use for a car. This family member mostly bicycled and used public transit; therefore, the gas, insurance and maintenance of the cars were not that person's responsibility. Another person worked at home and required a very fast internet connection and fully paid for it even though other members of the family used the connection. It comes down to individual needs and a family's willingness to accommodate those needs.

Families must decide in advance what seems most fair and equitable. In the case of things such as heat, lights and water should everyone pay an equal amount or proportional to their income? An equal amount seems to penalize the person with lower income. But what if that person took a job that paid a lower rate because it was a job they would love and be happy with? In a multi-income home, that choice is easier to make. In a line family each and every person does not have to earn money. Family members who do earn a paycheck might choose a career that they love but pays less because they have a stable line family living situation with multiple wage earners. Teaching is a prime example of work that is done out of a commitment to help students rather than an attempt to maximize financial gain. We believe that teachers should be paid more, but the reality now is that teaching is a calling to service. So, let's say a family member is making less than they could but is fulfilled by their work. Should that person pay an equal amount to the utilities fund? We don't know. These are your questions to answer with your line family. Make sure you get to these issues early and be ready to revisit the issues if they don't seem to be working for everyone. Remember to be flexible.

Real Property Ownership

We discuss this in detail in Chapter 8, Owning Real Property. All of our subject families owned their homes. Each family had a single property owner or a legally married couple as owners in the beginning. In only one case was a third person added to the mortgage. That person is contributing to the monthly house payment. There are various tools available for including another family member in the legal ownership of real property. With a large line family we suggest that you strongly consider having all of the partners jointly own or control the family property. When only one or two people own the land and buildings, there is a significant power shift to the sole owners. They are taking the financial risk and would probably feel that as the owners they should have final say as to how the property is used, maintained and developed.

Departing Family Members

It is a sad fact that not all relationships work out. Of all the families we interviewed, only one had a mechanism in place for departing members.

It is a corporate structure that allows for reimbursement of most of the money that the person invested in the family. Because that could be a substantial amount, the agreement sets out a payment plan. A new line family would be particularly susceptible to hardship should one departing member demand full and immediate payment. Therefore, rather than one lump sum, repayments would most likely be made in installments in order to not harm the financial stability of the family.

It is our feeling that a family member needs to be fairly compensated if the relationship ends. They have put money, labor and other talents into the family while a member. It would not be fair for a person to have nothing if they leave and no one should feel trapped because they can't afford to leave. This is one of those things that should be noted when new members are added. It is like a prenuptial agreement. Both individuals and the family need to be protected.

Last Will and Testament

At least 4 of the 5 families have wills of mutual benefit. It means as each member dies, their property is passed on to the surviving members of the family. Our feeling about this is that wills are not enough. You can read what happened to the Vanderbilts in the book *Fortune's Children*. They were once the richest family in the world. The Vanderbilt's problems stemmed from a lack of knowledge about how to manage money over multiple generations. This, combined with trying to use only wills to control the family fortune, led in part to their financial downfall. Legal tools such as limited liability companies and trusts help make a will stronger and less vulnerable to legal challenges. The richest families in the world manage their money; they don't divide it up with wills. This is discussed in greater detail in Chapters 5 and 8, Finances and Owning Real Property.

Elon's Opinion on Household Management

How do you feel about doing chores around the house? I'm afraid that I have a tendency to put off doing cleaning, when I can. That is especially true of chores that I have to do alone. For that reason, I prefer doing housework as part of a team. I find that when I have people with whom to do jobs, and we turn on some music and dance and/or sing while we do it, the work is done almost before we know it. Connections between the members of the group are often strengthened by working together, as well. Sometimes there is a person that I have a tendency to fight with whenever I am on the same team with them. I find that there are two things I can do (1) work to resolve the issues between us that cause friction or, (2) try to avoid being on the same team with them. In a line family, or any group where there is frequent contact between any two members of the group, solution number one is much more likely to increase group harmony. Therefore, that is by far my preferred solution.

CHAPTER FIVE

Finances

Their whole civil policy was averse to the concentration of power in the hands of any single individual, but inclined to the opposite principle of division among a number of equals.

Bruce Johansen
writing in *Forgotten Founders* about the Iroquois
Confederacy of Native Americans

Shack is rich;
the white man who signs his check is wealthy.
Wealth is multigenerational.

Chris Rock,
from Drugs, Donuts and Wealth
on the Never Scared album.

Finance is a huge topic that covers spending, saving and investing. One additional topic for your line family is handling family money over multiple generations. But before we go on you must understand WE ARE NOT LAWYERS OR FINANCIAL ADVISORS and that WE DO NOT GIVE LEGAL ADVICE! WE DO NOT GIVE FINANCIAL ADVICE. We are giving you information so that you will have an idea about some of the tools that are available to you and your family. We strongly suggest that you seek advice from a poly friendly attorney and financial advisor. With your help we will be posting a list of poly friendly professionals on www.line-family.info/CALF_companion/.

A few of the tools we want you to know about includes wills, revocable living trusts, joint tenancy with right of survivorship, advance healthcare directives (aka living wills) and powers of attorney. Our goal is to let you know that these tools exist. We will discuss when and how these tools might be used. There are more legal and financial tools available than what are covered here. We just want to get you started. These discussions are not intended to replace legal advice from an attorney licensed to practice law in your state. Laws differ from state to state. Laws also change from year to year and sometimes get altered by court decisions. Lawyers are paid to keep up with these changes. As with lawyers and doctors, there are many types of financial advisers. If you can, find professionals who are comfortable working with polyamorous people.

Problems with Wills

We are not big fans of using a will by itself for the management of personal and communal property. To demonstrate this we would like to show you what would happen to a typical poly quad as the partners die. This example quad has one legally married pair and two other partners.

1. Let's say one partner of the married couple dies first. This situation is generally pretty simple with the surviving spouse getting all

or most the community property or marital property.

2. For the sake of brevity let's say that two of the remaining partners die in a tandem surfing accident. The court looks at the wills and finds all the property goes to the last partner. So far so good, if a bit sad.

3. Eventually the last partner dies. With no surviving poly family partners, the secondary beneficiaries collect the loot. It is possible that the court will liquidate the real property (land, and improvements) and convert it to cash for the final distribution barring instruction to the contrary in the will.

4. Perhaps this person had a couple of favorite charities that got bequests. Maybe there are 3 or 4 distant blood relatives who will also receive goods and/or monies. If the various monies are small enough (under 2-million dollars in Washington State) there is no estate tax as of 2014. A person's estate is required to pay taxes if its combined gross assets and prior taxable gifts exceeded $5,430,000 in 2015. Only the dollars over the stated amount are taxed. This is what we call a classy problem. In Washington State, if you receive a 2-million dollar inheritance from a 5-million dollar estate – no estate taxes are collected by either the state of Washington or the Federal Government in 2014.

5. So, the accumulated wealth of this poly family (let's say 1 home free and clear and 2 homes with good equity plus savings, investments and personal property) is scattered among 6 or more beneficiaries. This means that the collective economic power of the family is diluted.

The fact is, when a family's money (cash, property, investment, etc.) increase, the family's economic power increases faster. A simple example is the power to borrow money. Let's say you want to borrow $100,000 to buy some raw land for investment purposes. If you need 10% down that is $10,000. That means you have borrowed $90,000. If you double the down payment to $20,000 you now have the power to borrow $180,000 and purchase twice as much land. An initial $20,000 investment can generate at least twice the potential profit of a $10,000 down payment.

Another factor is collateral. The more you have, the better the loan terms you can negotiate. The term for all of this is leverage. The more money you have the more power you have to perform economic activity. And this power is multiplied as your family accumulates financial assets.

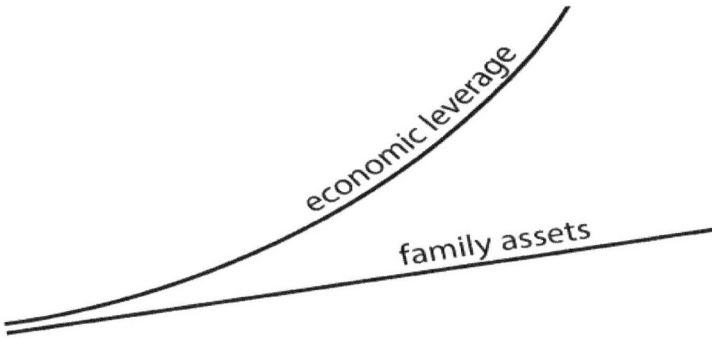

economic leverage

family assets

Divide these assets with a will and the economic power disappears quickly. We think this is a big part of the reason that most low- and middle-class families stay low- and middle-class. These are not the rules that the wealthy and powerful live by. Wealthy families use other financial tools to manage, distribute and control money. Various types of trusts are one set of powerful tools that we will look at.

Here's the secret that is in plain view, when Mr. and Mrs. Gotcash pass away, the family fortune is not carved up by wills. Family businesses stay in the family. Family investments fund trusts to support family members. The wealth is managed – never chopped up and distributed among the surviving family members.

To be fair, the above example quad family is more about the limits of a "horizontal poly family" meaning all the partners are of a similar age. Even using trusts, LLCs and other legal entities, this family would still end after the last person died. Let's not dwell on single-generation families since this book is about multigenerational line families.

Wills do have their place. With little up-front costs, a will is an easy tool you can use to establish a guardianship for minor children. Wills are often used to set up a testamentary trust that provides monetary support for a child. This type of trust is only created when the will goes into effect. The will describes the details of the trust and funds the trust from the monies in the estate. Surviving pets can be provided for with their own testamentary trust.

The probate process generates a lot of complaints, but probate does extend protection for your estate against mismanagement, fraud and embezzlement. However, the transfer of businesses, investment accounts and other assets would most likely be covered in the operating agreements of a family's LLCs and corporate entities (see Chapter 11, Cohabitation Arrangements for details). Your lawyer can assist you in determining what issues to cover in a will and what issues would be best handled by other legal tools.

An example of a powerful legal tool for managing property is the Transfer on Death Deed or Beneficiary Deed. This is a relatively new way to transfer real property ownership while avoiding probate and challenges to a will. As of 2014 the states of Arizona, Arkansas, Colorado, District of Columbia, Hawaii, Illinois, Indiana, Kansas, Minnesota, Missouri, Montana, Nebraska, Nevada, New Mexico, North Dakota, Ohio, Oklahoma, Oregon, Virginia, Washington and Wisconsin allow this practice. It looks like it might be a good tool for poly families (though probably not appropriate for line families). There are other tools for managing property that we will discuss that might be better suited to multigenerational line families.

Trusts

Put not your trust in money,
but put your money in trust.

Oliver Wendell Holmes, Jr., 1841-1935
(Poet and Associate Justice
U.S. Supreme Court, 1902-1932)

What is a trust? Here's what the IRS says, "In general, a trust is a relationship in which one person holds title to property, subject to an obligation to keep or use the property for the benefit of another. A trust is formed under state law. You may wish to consult the law of the state in which the organization is organized."

Is this an example of the new warm and fuzzy IRS that says you "may" want to consult your state laws? We don't know why or how you would avoid consulting your state laws when determining the types of trust accounts that would be right for your line family. Again, we urge you to get assistance from your bank, credit union, investment professional, attorney, etc.

Basic Elements of a Trust:

Typically there are four elements involved in a trust account:

First is the person who has the property that is to be placed in the trust. Depending on the laws and customs of your state this person may be referred to as the: settler, trustor, grantor, creator, founder or donor. Of all these words "donor" makes the most sense to us and we will use that term when discussing trusts in this book.

Second is the beneficiary, the person who controls and receives the benefits of the property. Control means that the beneficiary decides how the property is to be used and benefits from that use. If the beneficiary controls farmland, the decision about the types of crops planted and the profits (or losses) from that crop are the beneficiary's. While the beneficiary controls the property, the property is owned by the trust.

Third is the trustee, the person or business who holds the property for the beneficiary. Note: the donor can also be the trustee.

Fourth is the property, or corpus, of the trust. A trust must control some type of tangible asset.

Now that you know what a trust is, here is a partial list of what can go into a trust:

> *Real estate, art, gold, cash, investment accounts (stocks, mutual funds, bonds), T-bills, annuities, life insurance, collectibles, personal possessions...*

Pretty much anything of value can be protected and managed in a trust.

Types of Trusts

When a person dies, a trust can be part of the will. This type of trust is called a "Testamentary Trust" and is used in managing an individual's property upon death. As such, this type of trust is usually not relevant to a discussion about your line family's finances. We include this because you should know about your options in managing your personal estate.

We are interested in trusts made by living persons for living persons (in Latin: inter vivos). (What, you expected to talk about law without learning a little Latin?) This type of trust is divided into "revocable" trusts and "irrevocable" trusts. Trusts are often used instead of wills because a will can be contested and trusts normally can't. Also trusts are generally not part of any probate proceeding.

Revocable Living Trust

One huge advantage of this type of trust is spelled out in the name; you, as the donor, can revoke your living trust. You can also modify it if circumstances change. You can sell your property, if the need arises, without the permission of anyone named as a beneficiary of your living trust. Beneficiaries of your trust don't even need to be told that they are beneficiaries. All the real and personal property covered by your living trust should pass to the beneficiaries without going through probate.

A living trust also provides security and privacy because the document does not have to be filed with any government agency. A trust is not a public document. Only the donor and trustee (who can be the same person) know what assets are included in the trust. The trust document can authorize a successor trustee if the original trustee is not available or is not able to fulfill the role.

All the assets of the trust remain in the donor's control until death or incapacitation. If the donor becomes incapacitated a court can order a conservatorship (guardianship) for the donor's financial affairs. A conservatorship is created when a person is judged unable to manage their basic needs for food, clothing and shelter. This can happen due to mental issues such as dementia or Alzheimer's disease. Any mental disability that prevents a person from making reasonable financial decisions can be grounds for a court to assign a conservatorship. A conservator assignment can also be created in cases of profound physical disability. However a donor's incapacity does not automatically cause a conservatorship to be established. A donor can take steps to avoid a conservatorship by setting up a power of attorney for financial matters. Also note that a judgment of incapacity does not trigger any transfer of property in a trust from the donor to the beneficiary.

Power of Attorney (Attorney in Fact)

Mentally competent people are able to create powers of attorney for a variety of issues. In creating a power of attorney you give someone you trust the authority to act on your behalf. You can limit this power to a time when you become incapable of managing your estate because of physical sickness or mental incapacity. Should you become incapacitated and you have no power of attorney in place, a conservatorship can be granted by a court and you will have little say about who becomes your guardian. To appoint a conservator, the court will look to a legal spouse or blood relatives. Anyone not related by blood will probably not be selected by the court. Currently poly families have no legal protection unless everyone takes the time to get the appropriate power of attorney paperwork filled out.

Other Types of Trusts

Educational Trusts can be used to fund a child's education. IRS guidelines regarding the gift tax is discussed in Chapter 6, Children. The IRS provides exemptions from the gift tax for educational gifts and in calculating the tax-free amounts you can give to a child in a single year. A trust can be set up so that the money is doled out periodically to pay expenses such as tuition, books and room and board while the child is in school.

Special Needs Trusts are usually set up to meet the needs of a disabled child or adult. Funding for these types of trusts can come from a child's parents through their life insurance. When the parents die, the insurance money is used to fund the trust. Another funding mechanism is a lawsuit where the injured person receives a cash settlement. A trust is set up funded by the settlement to support the injured person and manage the money.

Managing money is one of the strengths of trust accounts. If you have businesses that are generating income for your line family's holding company, you might want to use trust accounts to pay the pensions of your older members who are working part time or are retired. The trust keeps the retirement money separate from the business. Should a business fail, the retirement money stays safe and available for the retirees.

Ever hear the stories about millionaires who have gone bankrupt two or three times, only to return to wealth and power? We wondered how that is done. It turns out that trusts are often used in these cases. Discretionary trusts are tools that can be used to hide or isolate property from creditors. Some methods are legal and some are not. It is not our intent to go into the details of illegal uses of this tool. We mention it only to demonstrate the power of trusts.

One Billionaire's Story

By 1998 Bill Bartmann owned and ran the largest debt collection company in the United States. Bill and his wife had formed a company called Commercial Financial Services (CFS) in 1986. His business model was ingenious. In the beginning the company bought the debts of failed banks from the Federal Deposit Insurance Corporation (FDIC). They bought the debt for 2 cents on the dollar and collected an average of 10 cents on the dollar. Next the company bought bad real estate loans from failed saving and loan companies, collected what they could and made a good profit.

In 1993 CFS started buying bad credit card debt. Credit card loans that are overdue by 180 days are worth nothing on a bank's books. Bartmann's company would buy these bad debts for pennies on the dollar. Everything CFS could collect above the amount they had paid to the banks was profit. Bartmann also started bundling the debt and converting it into bonds, selling them as investments. In its heyday the company had thousands of collectors sitting at desks working out deals where the company would collect an average 30 cents for every 10 cents used to purchase the bad debt. In the mid '90s it was claimed that Bartmann's company owned about half of the US delinquent credit card debt.

In October of 1998 the vice president of CFS, Jay Jones plead guilty to one count of conspiracy. Jones created a shell company – using his own money – to buy millions of dollars in loans from CFS. CFS then recorded the sales as collections. This was done by Jones to insure the company's bond rating. Bartmann claims he knew nothing about the scam and that none of his money was used by the shell company to make the purchases.

CFS was ruined. The company couldn't sell any bonds. In July 1999 the company went bankrupt. Investors sued Bartmann and CFS. Jones copped a plea and did some time in jail. Bartmann was indicted on 57 felony counts. He filed for bankruptcy. In court he was acquitted of all 57 charges.

Eleven years later (2011) Bartmann formed a new credit card collection company. Somehow he managed to find 25 million dollars for his new business. Bartmann claims that a book he had written and the lecture circuit had done very well for him. (This book's authors are on the wrong lecture circuit.)

Stories of fabulously wealthy people who have "lost it all" and then returned to great wealth are not that uncommon. While Bartmann's story of recovery might be totally factual, we are guessing that there might be more to the story than a successful book and lecture series. Perhaps he found an angel investor or two interested in the kind of returns Bartmann made in the '90s. Angel investors are a perfectly legitimate source of business capital. Another common tactic that has been used by many wealthy individuals is the use of trusts to shelter money, sort of a rainy-day fund. Since trusts are private, they are difficult for lawyers to discover. For billionaires, putting a few million into trusts would hardly put a crimp in their lifestyle. We are not saying that is what Bartmann did. All we are saying is that it has been done by others in the past.

Trusts are only one method of sheltering money. In a December 2012 Town and Country article, "What Money? Where?" author Tome Acitelli describes how wealthy people also use LLCs, Private Foundations, Agents (Attorney in Fact), and Write-Downs to make themselves a less inviting financial target for lawyers looking for deep pockets to sue. Mr. Acitelli seems very sympathetic to the plight of the "1 percent." The secondary title for his article is, "In the Age of the Occupiers, There are Several Legal Methods that the Embattled 1 Percent Are Using to Hide their Purchases and Acquisitions."

For those who may not remember, the Occupy Movement, which was referred to in the above quote, was an international protest against the gross economic inequalities that were found in many countries. The international protest was sparked by the Occupy Wall Street protests starting on September 17, 2011. While Mr. Acitelli makes a blanket statement about the legality of using all these tools to shelter money, we would not go so far. The legalities of such practices are up to the laws and courts of wherever you happen to live. We are describing some powerful tools. They can be used in a reasonable and legal manner. But like all powerful tools, they can also be used in questionable circumstances or for downright illegal purposes.

Trusts are a powerful tool for managing money over multiple generations. Businesses organized under your line family's holding company (possibly an LLC) can be funded through trusts. Trusts can manage the profits from family businesses to benefit all of the family members. Trusts help your family live by one of the rules of the wealthy;

Own nothing and control everything.

John D. Rockefeller

Using a family LLC as a trustee is one way to control and manage multiple trusts. It might, however, not be the best alternative for family privacy because the details of an LLC are public information. We can't say this enough – consult an attorney.

Advanced Health Care Directives
(Also known as Living Wills)

You are in a car accident and end up in a coma. How do you want your medical care to be handled? You're in no condition to sign insurance forms or treatment authorizations; but, if you have an advanced health care directive (AHCD) in place, the person you named as your representative will be able to convey your wishes. An AHCD only goes into effect when you become incapacitated with no prospect for immediate recovery.

Powers of Attorney

A power of attorney allows a friend, family member, business partner or other person to perform legal actions for you. The person to whom you give a power of attorney is known as an agent or an attorney in fact. Powers of attorney (POAs) can be limited or durable. Also the kinds of responsibilities your agent performs are spelled out in the document creating the POA.

Limited Powers of Attorney

You may want to set up powers of attorney for situations such as the car accident scenario described above. Your AHCD representative has little or no control over your estate, investments or business interests. While you are in a coma, the person you appointed with your financial power of attorney can act in financial matters for you. Your attorney in fact can stabilize your portfolio if you are an active trader and make sure your financial obligations are resolved. Your attorney in fact can also act for you in other matters of law as long as the power of attorney document permits that authority. It is best if your attorney in fact is someone who already has familiarity with your business affairs. You also might execute a limited POA for general financial matters such as bills, selling personal or real property or signing a contract when you're travelling in remote areas away from a means of communication (it could happen). Maybe you just want to take a real vacation and let the world turn without you for a month or two while you write the great line family novel. Having an attorney in fact can save you a lot of money.

Let's look a little closer at this helpful tool. The financial power of attorney described above is a form of limited POA. It can be limited in time from when you are incapacitated to when you are well again. It is also limited in scope. It is about overseeing your financial affairs. It authorizes your attorney in fact to make financial decision about your investment funds, real estate or any other issue authorized by the POA.

If you are not married to any of the members of your line family, it would be especially important to consider creating medical POAs, in case of emergencies. A medical POA is another type of limited POA. Each member of your family can give multiple people medical POAs. The POA will let your family members visit you anytime while you are in a hospital; visiting hours don't apply to a person with a medical POA. You will probably want to designate a primary medical representative if you have multiple medical POAs. The primary attorney in fact will be responsible for making sure the instructions in your health care directive are followed. Note: You should probably create a separate POA document for each person that you want to give access to your medical information and have a say in your care.

Durable Powers of Attorney

It's durable in that there is no stated time limit or conditions that end the POA except for the death of the grantor. At that time the person designated as the executor of the estate would take over. Giving someone a durable POA should not be taken lightly. As with limited POAs, a durable POA will detail the type of actions that can be taken on your behalf. Usually a person with your POA can sign binding contracts in your name, incur debts in your name or anything else that would require your signature. However we don't think your agent could get married for you without your involvement. All of this is to say you need to really trust the person to whom you give a durable power of attorney.

Investments

Investments are a key to multigenerational financial planning. There are four asset classes you can invest in. They are businesses, real estate, commodities and paper. Business as an asset means both full and partial ownership of the business itself. However, it does not include owning common stock in a business. That is considered a paper asset along with other stocks, mutual funds, insurance, notes, etc.

To be considered an investment, real property and the improvements to the land must reflect and support family businesses. Real estate is an asset when it is producing a positive cash flow such as a rental property. Just owning real property does not make it an asset. The real estate you use for your primary residence is a liability. Your primary residence is probably not producing a positive cash flow even if you are renting out a room. But what if your primary residence is paid off? That's great, but you still owe yearly taxes, incur maintenance costs and pay premiums for insuring the property.

Commodities can be marketable things such as precious metals, petroleum products, food crops and so on. These are tangible products that are bought and sold to satisfy wants and needs. These products have no differing value based on a brand association. For example, refined gold from Mexico is the same as refined gold from Russia. Tools for investing in commodities include futures contracts, exchange traded funds and exchange traded notes. You can also use paper, stocks and mutual funds to invest in commodities. Please see your financial advisor for details.

Using paper to invest in commodities such as gold or food crops is one of the ways that the four asset classes often get blended into one another. Another type of blended investing is buying real estate for creating a business. Even though you only have four basic investment classes, things can quickly get very complex.

Reserve Accounts

Some of your line family's money can also be kept in one or more reserve accounts. These accounts are separate from the family checking account that is used for groceries, fuel, utilities and other daily and monthly expenses. Family reserve accounts can be created to pay for unscheduled household repairs, appliance replacement, major vehicle expenses, education, vacations, property taxes, events, parties, child support and so on. Since this is all family money, could it all be kept in one account? Yes, and that would probably be a good idea because there would probably be fewer fees for setting up one account versus many. However with one account someone must be willing to manage it and divide the money into whatever sub categories your family chooses.

More Investments

A Reminder: We are not investment counselors.

In this section we will mention a few basic investment strategies and instruments. We suggest that you study the subject for yourself. Unbiased classes can be difficult to find. Always be aware of an instructor's bias. This is particularly true if they represent an investment firm. Books on investing can also have a bias. Check out who wrote it and what house published the book. Also check out the reviews.

Before you empty out your savings or checking accounts for your investment portfolio, remember that it is always good to have a reasonable amount of ready cash available. This is usually accommodated by maintaining a checking account and/or savings account and making cash withdrawals when needed from an ATM or using a debit card. We vigorously stress using caution with credit cards. If you use one to collect airline miles, for instance, one option is to have an automatic payment system in place if you are comfortable with that type of set up. Otherwise, you must have someone in charge of paying the credit card bill off every month. Either way, keep an adequate amount of money in the account used to pay off the credit card each month.

An important number in the world of savings, investments and loans is 72. If you divide an interest rate into 72, you will find out how many years it would take to double your money. Divide 72 by your credit card rate to find out how fast your debt doubles if you are only paying the minimum each month. Look at this example of how long it would take to double your money in a passbook savings account earning 1%. One goes into 72, 72 times. That means it will take seventy-two years to double your money – that is not very good. At 10% interest your money doubles in a little less than 7 years 2 months. On average, 2014 credit card rates have been floating between 13% and 23% for people with good credit. Divide 72 by 13 and you get a doubling every 5.5 years and 23% doubles in just over 3.1 years. If you don't have a good credit score, your credit card interest rate can go much higher.

Credit Cards can be Hazardous to Your Financial Health

We found a card (for people with poor credit) that charges 29.99% and has an annual fee of $125 to $180. In addition to the high rates and fees, your card could start charging you interest on the day you make a purchase. It means that paying the bill promptly at the end of the month does not keep you from paying interest. Don't let yourself be tempted by a low initial interest rate. Make sure that when the introductory rate is through that you are not stuck with a financial leech such as the one described here.

The lesson in all this is to have enough cash – but not too much – sitting in checking or savings accounts to cover regular living expenses. You also do not want to have a balance carried from one month to the next on a credit card. Credit card debt that is not paid off every month is a net loser – a liability.

Warnings about credit cards and debit cards: "Plastic" is not always safe. In your favorite search engine enter the words "credit card skimmer." You will not only learn of the large amounts of money stolen from personal bank accounts using captured card numbers and PINs, you will also be able to buy skimming equipment of your very own. We suspect that several of these websites are probably official sting operations and we say good hunting to them. Another interesting web search can be done at www.usa.gov/. Search "Credit Card Fraud" and "Debit Card Scams". It lists several other interesting methods for siphoning money from your plastic. Also, credit card companies themselves have not always played fair with consumers.

Credit Score Roulette
(Know the house rules)

If you want a good credit rating you need a credit history. A credit card can be a good way to develop that history. However, how you use your credit card has a significant effect on your credit score. As it turns out, paying your credit card bill in full every month is not currently a negative for the credit reporting agencies. Maxine Sweet, VP of Public Education for Experian discusses that issue on their website (http://www.experian.com/blogs/ask-experian/). "Balances on credit cards are usually updated by your creditors once a month and typically reflect the balance in your billing statement. If you tend to have high balances on your revolving accounts throughout the month, it's likely that those balances will be reflected on your credit report when the score is calculated. In addition to how much you owe, one of the most important factors in credit scores is how close your balances are to your credit limits."

Ms. Sweet goes on to indicate that the balance on your card is taken once a month and not usually when you have just paid off the balance. It is a negative factor for your credit score if your card balance is close to the card limit. She called it a "utilization ratio." For your credit score, it doesn't matter if you pay it in full every month. It matters that you pay at least the minimum every month and that you do not have a high utilization ratio. One way to get a better utilization ratio is to get a higher limit on your card. Another way is to split your expenses between two cards. For these strategies to be successful, you must not increase your spending.

Another interesting bit of news is that debit cards do not help your credit score. Most debit cards can be run as credit cards. In this case, the credit bill is paid automatically. Just make sure your account balance is high enough to cover the credit bill. Credit cards are handy for quick cash when a sudden expense comes up such as traveling in the desert southwest and you manage to blow out two or more of your tires at once driving on a bad road.

Remember that credit reporting agencies change their criteria for rating consumer credit. Paying off your card every month used to be a bad thing for your credit score. Now they care about your utilization rations and that you pay some monthly payment whether it is the minimum amount, a full payment or something in-between. What we have told you about credit ratings will probably be different in 10 or 20 years. The good news is that you can find out a lot about their credit rating practices on the reporting agency's websites and by contacting them directly and asking questions.

You can get into trouble with credit cards and can find yourself dealing with a collection agency. Collection agencies can be employed by the bank before the debt is written off, or the bank can sell their debt after writing it off their books. Either way, if you get into a situation where you are being contacted by a collection agency, it is important to get some information. Ask if the collection agency is working directly for the bank. If they say yes, you should call the bank to confirm that information. That means a portion of anything you pay to the agency will go to the bank. If the collection agency has purchased the written off debt, the agency is not working for the bank and will keep all the money they collect from you. In either case, ask if the money they collect from you is reported to the credit bureaus as paid debt? If not, the payments you make to the collection agency will not help your credit rating.

Here's another important note: Get rich quick schemes almost always work – for the person promoting them, not the person that gets involved with one. Even if the thief who set up the scam is caught, the victims rarely get back the money they lost. Type "Bernie Madoff" into a web browser for a good example of a major scam. Investors who lost money recovered only 14.4 cents on the dollar.

Diversity is a time-tested concept for investment portfolios. There are many safe monetary instruments in which to place your money. One of the safest is US Treasury Bills (aka T-Bills). T-Bills are bonds sold by the federal government. The return on investment (ROI) is not great, but it is better than a pass-book savings account. The only way T-Bills don't pay off is if the U.S. Government collapses. In that case you will have much more to worry about than some dollars tied up in T-Bills.

Certificates of Deposit

Also known as CDs, these are fixed interest rate instruments that pay more than most passbook savings but usually not enough to keep up with inflation. They tie up your money for some specific period of time, generally from 3 or 6 months up to multiple years. We think that money tied up in low-interest-rate paper is not the best (or even safest) use of your family's money. If we recommended specific investments (but we don't) we would hesitate to recommend CDs. We are just telling you about them because they are so common.

Precious Metals and Coins

As a stable and universal means of exchange, gold coins are about as real as money gets. The US Mint produces silver, platinum and gold coins. You can buy uncirculated precious metal proof coins directly from the Mint. That way you know exactly what you are buying. Be aware that there are two major types of precious-metal coins, proof and bullion. Proof coins are polished coins that generally commemorate an event or person. The price of the coin is usually much higher than the price of the metal in the coin. A bullion coin's value is based on the amount and quality of the precious metal in the coin.

The Mint does not sell bullion coins directly. However at the U.S. Mint website you can find a list of "authorized gold bullion coin dealers." Iowa has only one authorized dealer, New York has 15 and California has 55. (We just found those statistics oddly interesting.)

Other ways of investing in precious metals include certificates, stock in mining companies, mutual funds that include or specialize in precious metals and metals futures. (We do not consider futures a basic investment instrument and they will not be discussed here.) See a broker or certified investment counselor about these investments. For commodities investing you might want to check out www.goldsilver.com and www.wealthcycles.com.

Gold is an investment in long-term security. Over the long term gold does not tend to increase or decrease in value. There are short term increases and drops in the price. But when it comes to buying power, an ounce of gold will buy the same amount of goods or services in New York City that it bought 200 years ago. For example, an ounce of gold will buy you the same type and quality of a man's suit now that it did two centuries ago. Gold is one of the stable means of maintaining wealth that has been used by the economic elite class for centuries. We don't see that changing in the near future in spite of gold's price fluctuations.

Individual Stocks

Investing in individual stocks is a good way to make - or lose - a fair amount of money. Stock conveys an ownership position in a company – a very small ownership position. Stocks can provide income from dividends paid to the stockholder. If the company is doing well, the dividend is high. If the company is doing poorly, there is little or no dividend paid. When a stock's price is higher than what your family paid for it, it may be sold for a profit. There are other things that can be done with individual stocks such as "puts" and "calls" but they are beyond the scope of this book.

Stocks also add personal emotion into the equation. Most people don't want to admit they have made a mistake. Holding stocks for the long haul is generally a good thing, but holding stock in a company that makes photography film while photography was going digital was not wise. This is why having a financial advisor for your stock portfolio makes sense. It takes a lot of the emotion out of the game. And it is a game. Don't go too heavily into stocks unless you have a huge tolerance for risk.

And now a cautionary tale: Richard bought Amazon stock early and it almost doubled. Then on July 27, 2001 the tech-bubble burst with Microsoft, Real Networks, Sun Microsystems and other major tech companies laying off at least 10% of their employees. Tech stock prices started sliding fast. Richard had loans that came due and he had to sell his Amazon stock at a substantial loss. Of course the stock recovered, but that was little comfort. Luckily he didn't sell his Apple stock. On average he is way ahead but being in debt and not having cash available cost him a large profit.

It's not just us, most investment counselors we have seen on TV, read in magazines and talked to personally suggest that individuals do not invest heavily (or at all) in individual stocks. The one exception they make is that if you really know the business, you might put a small percentage of your portfolio in one or two stocks. Avoid hunches or "hot tips" from friends or coworkers. More often than not hunches and tips do not pay off.

Bonds

Bonds differ from stocks in that bonds are loans. When you buy a bond you are loaning your money for a specific amount of interest to be paid back along with the principal. Your return on investment and the maturity date are fixed on simple bonds. Normally bonds pay interest every 6 months. That means bonds can deliver a reliable income while not risking the initial money invested.

You can invest in bonds with interest rates that move up or down based on a reference rate. There are also bonds that have "put" or "call" options, but those topics get too involved for the scope of this book.

Bond Funds

Bond funds invest in multiple bonds. It might be a diverse fund or one that invests only in municipal bonds, corporate bonds or any other specialty type of bond.

Mutual Funds

A mutual fund is an investment tool used by money managers in an investment company. Mutual funds pool the money of many investors. Managers of a mutual fund can invest in a broad range of instruments including bonds, stocks, short-term money market paper, etc. We think this is a good way for a small investor to diversify their holdings. If you really want to invest in stocks, you can do it through a mutual fund that invests in a sector of the stock market you are interested in.

Indexed Funds

Common indexed funds invest in the S&P 500, S&P 1,000, the Nikkie Average and other large groups of stocks. Indexed funds can specialize in currency trading and bond funds. This is another way to spread risk over a large number of instruments.

Universal Life Insurance

Mike Flannery is a financial advisor for this book. We have Mike to thank for everything we got right on financial matters. Anything we got wrong is our fault. In talking with Mike he explained a little about IRS code 7702 that states you can save money in a life insurance plan and take it out tax exempt. An indexed universal life policy is indexed to a fund such as the S&P 500 but it is not in the stock market. It generally has a floor of 0% and ceiling of 12% meaning you can't lose money when the market is low. When the market is up, gains of up to 12% are possible.

There is much more to discuss here. Mike talked about using a universal life insurance plan as a bank from which you can borrow money. You pay interest on the loan, but you are paying it to yourself rather than a bank. It is one of Mike's favorite retirement account tools. You can find Mike's contact information at www.line-family.info. He has been working with the alternative lifestyle community for quite a while and is in full support of the non-monogamous community.

Annuities

Annuities are a tool that a line family can use in setting up its members for retirement. An annuity is a contract between a financial institution and the purchaser. The purchaser funds the annuity with either a lump sum payment or regular payments, usually monthly. These payments are a fixed amount for a fixed period of time. The financial institution invests the purchaser's money. Starting at a predetermined date, the financial institution makes regular payments back to the purchaser. These payments can continue for a fixed period of time, usually 20 years or for the life of the purchaser. The payment can be a fixed amount or vary with the success of the financial institution's investment returns.

A variety of annuities are available including: deferred, equity, fixed, immediate, indexed, variable, etc. It all depends on the goals of the purchaser and the amount of risk the purchaser is willing to take. Insurance companies sell most of the annuities purchased in the United States. The payments, or distributions, made to the purchaser must be claimed on the purchaser's income tax. The taxable amount is figured by subtracting the money that the purchaser initially paid into the annuity.

Check with a tax professional to get the details.

Real Property

Owning real property – land and the permanent improvements thereupon – for your primary residence provides security and generally delivers lower long-term living expenses when compared to renting. You're going to pay money to live someplace, you might as well be paying some of the money to yourself. However, real property used for your primary residence is a liability because it probably has a negative cash flow even if it has no mortgages.

Please note that if family property is owned by only a few individuals in the family, an unequal balance of power exists because the property owners are liable for the risk incurred by any family member's use of the property. We believe it is better if real property is owned by the family as a whole. There are many methods for group-ownership of land. We go into more detail about group ownership of real property in Chapter 8, Owning Real Property.

Real property is an investment when it is used to turn a profit. Land is needed for retail space. Land can also be used to grow cash crops. A lot of land is needed for an airport. You can use a piece of residential property as an investment by making it a rental property.

Real Property is not just the raw land. Real property is also the permanent improvements to the land. For example, an in-ground swimming pool is real property – an above ground pool is not. Buildings with foundations are real property as are trees, wells and anchored fencing. Portable sheds built from kits, fruit that has fallen from a tree and self-standing fencing are not real property. Any property that is not real property is personal property.

For more information on investing, we've been recommending Robert Kiyosaki's book Unfair Advantage. For more details on investing in the new economy we've also been recommending his early books, Rich Dad, Poor Dad and The Cashflow Quadrant.

Family Business

We believe that family businesses can play an important role in developing a stable and strong multigenerational line family (unless you become the royal family of some nation that produces a fabulously valuable export; great work if you can get it). Drive through any business district and you will see all sorts of business ideas. One of the first "problems" people make for themselves when thinking about starting a business, is that they don't have any original ideas. We'll tell you a little secret, Ben and Jerry did not invent ice-cream. They started small and found that people would pay more for a clearly superior product.

Ask around in your family. Does anyone have passion and/ or knowledge about some product? If so, you might start a business producing a higher-quality version of the product. Conversely, a more economical (cheaper) version of the product might also have a ready market.

How about a service business? Twin Oakes, for example, has a thriving book-indexing business. Is there an artist in your family? How about starting a graphics design business? After looking at the talent that exists in your family, check out what your land can provide. One socially-responsible business would be growing heritage seeds. And if the world's monoculture crops failed, your family would still be producing food. Do you have room to board animals? Opportunities and ideas are everywhere.

Have a business brainstorming session at your next family meeting. A business that employs retired members of your family part time could be a great way to provide another family income stream. We have met several retired people who worked even when they didn't need to. Having a purpose and feeling like we are contributing is a human trait, which does not end at a forced retirement age. Now let's look at some of the details about forming either a family business or an individual family member's business.

Storefront Businesses

We are going to assume that you want to open a "brick and mortar" retail business. We are using this business model because it is the most expensive and complex type of business to start. Old sayings are old because they are humorous or tell a simple truth. "It takes money to make money" is not particularly funny, but when opening a retail business, it is the simple truth. Your proposed business will need a budget. Prospective lenders want to know what you are going to do with the money. Even if all the seed money comes from line family funds, a budget is as necessary as architectural drawings are when building a house. The budget will address issues such as the cost of leasing a store front. Other expenses include buying the furniture, displays, business machines and other equipment. What will it cost to stock your business with product? Will you have employees? If so, how many and what will you offer in pay and benefits? An important upfront cost to consider is your advertising expenses. Advertising expenses are one of the first business reserve accounts you might want to set up.

Reserve accounts are an important tool for managing money. These are a type of savings account used for emergencies, annual expenses and planned expenses. In business, reserve accounts are set up to pay things such as taxes, maintenance costs, insurance premiums, employee retirement, major equipment purchases, investor dividends and other expenses depending on the type of business. All reserve accounts are given a dollar value that indicates the amount needed to be fully funded. There is one final account that businesses like to have. Generally the money left over when all business expenses are paid and all reserve accounts are fully funded is the business's profit.

If you multiply your monthly expenses by 3 to 6 times, you will get the amount of dollars recommended for weathering most temporary financial troubles. Reserve accounts are funded with dollars or other liquid assets that can rapidly be changed into dollars. A mutual fund that pays an interest rate that beats the current inflation rate is a good idea. You might use a mutual fund that invests in short term paper. If you use a mutual fund for a reserve account, you should be able to retrieve money from the fund's brokerage in 2 to 3 days. One method for quick money transfers from a mutual fund into a business or family checking/ debit account is through an Automated Clearing House (ACH) transfer. An ACH transfer is done electronically between financial institutions in the United States. ACH transfers are safer and more convenient than handling cash or checks. Usually ACH transfers are much faster than having a brokerage cut a check, which you must go pick up and then deposit into the appropriate bank account where it takes a day or two to clear. ACH transfers are often free, but check the brokerage rules to make sure, preferably before you invest your money through their organization.

As described above, your emergency funds can be in accounts that are interest bearing, or not. Longer term investments can be used to fund reserve accounts for scheduled expenses such as taxes or lease payments. Interest generated from such accounts must be reported to the IRS. It will not affect your taxes much. However you manage it, it is important to have some cash set aside for unexpected expenses. Seek professional advice specific to your state.

Planning a Business

Another part of the blueprint for your new enterprise is a business plan. In today's fast paced world your business plan needs to be well organized and concise, in other words short and easy to read. One tip is to not make your reader guess at what you're saying. Avoid technical jargon, acronyms and buzzwords. Bullet points are a good organizational tool; just make sure that each bullet point is self-explanatory. Other useful graphic tools are photos and charts. Any graphics should be referenced in your text, preferably on the same page or on the facing page. Don't make your reader turn back and forth between pages if possible. You have probably used pie charts and bar charts (histograms) before. These charts are good for comparing figures. Your report might also use Gant charts. This type of chart is usually a horizontal line representing time. Use this chart to show the order and timing of milestones described in your business plan.

Now a brief course in document design: Don't make your business plan look like a ransom note with 7 or 8 different type styles, or fonts. Typically titles and headings use a sans-serif type such as Helvetica, Verdana or Arial. Type styles with serifs are generally used for the main text such as Bookman, Garamond or Century. (Serifs are the small decorative lines added as embellishments to the basic form of a character.) The text in the body of your business plan should be no smaller than 11 points and 12 points is probably better. The last tip in your beginning design class is to use white space. People do not read informational documents like they read novels. Make sure you have two or three blank horizontal spaces per page in your text. Each blank space should be the size of two or three lines of body text.

Your business plan needs to be shorter than 30 pages unless you use a lot of full-page photos. If you use large photos, in addition to helping to tell your business' story, they must excite the imagination. In a business plan your story starts with an executive summary. Wait, don't fire up the word processor yet. You will probably want to wait until you are finished writing your business plan before writing an executive summary. It is hard to summarize what you have not yet written. It will be the introduction and will mention the important points that you cover in your business plan. It is probably better to start out by writing a business description. It is fairly straight forward. Describe what you want to sell and what need or desire it fills. Also discuss how your business is different from other similar businesses. Maybe you are providing a premium quality version of a product or an economical alternative to similar products.

Define your audience. To whom are you going to sell your product? Analyze your intended customers and figure out in detail why they need or want what you are selling. Will it be a narrow product line like left handed personal grooming products or a broad range like a toy store? Using these examples, what is the product lifecycle of a hair brush or a child's toy? This can help you predict repeat business. Make sure to outline your marketing plans. These include your initial advertising campaign to let people know about your new business and the long-term plans that keep people coming to your store.

A financial projection is probably the most daunting part of a business plan. The expense side of the business is the easiest to calculate. First you add up all the money needed to just get the business ready to open the doors. This includes things such as initial stock, store furnishings, license fees, damage deposits and so on. Regular expenses include your monthly lease, money paid for wages and loan repayment schedule. Your prospective lender really wants to see that last item in your financial projection. Some expenses are variable such as utilities, but it is not too hard to come up with numbers. You can ask neighboring stores or contact the utility companies directly for information. The cost of replacing stock is where things get tough because you must come up with reasonable sales projections. We recommend getting assistance from your local Small Business Administration office to help you develop a realistic sales projection.

Another thing that lenders will consider is your knowledge of the product you are selling and any experience you have in similar businesses.

Review the jobs you have held and see what transferable skills might be applicable to your business idea. Have you ever managed anything that involved money and/or people such as a community theatre production, a charitable giving campaign, a political campaign, etc.? If so, that demonstrates that you can manage people and get complex projects done. Your skills and projects show a lender that you have a track record of accomplishments and knowledge that will help you succeed in your business. This is part of the human capital we talked about in Chapter 2, Capital.

Who are these prospective lenders we've been mentioning? Your line family's money is one source of potential funds if enough people are interested in your business idea. But what if this is a personal project which either didn't generate much enthusiasm in your family or that you want to pursue on your own? In that case, you are the first source of financing. Before anyone else will risk their money they will want to know about your commitment to the business. Loan companies and most individuals with money to lend will measure your commitment by the amount of personal money you are willing to invest. If your savings account is a little thin, you might look at your personal belongings that you no longer use for sources of money. Often sporting goods, from activities in which you no longer participate, can bring in some decent cash. Perhaps your mother did not throw out your old collection of comic books, sports trading cards or vinyl record albums. Those can be quite valuable. Your parent's attics and basements can be goldmines of saleable items.

Business Gets Personal
(Throwing out the middle man)

Social media and online culture has opened up new ways of doing business. One example is eBay. On this site there is no middle man between the seller and buyer of goods and specialty services. This is the basic concept of peer-to-peer lending (also known as "social lending"). It is similar to eBay in that individuals with money to loan make direct contact with people looking for loans. Peer-to-peer lending developed because of web technologies that allow collaboration between lots of people in diverse places. Facebook is just the most visible web tool available that enables collaborative efforts. Modern micro lending became a social tool in the mid '80s when people started lending small amounts of money to individuals in poor countries to start their own businesses. Now there is Prosper (www.prosper.com/) where individuals can search for loans from other individuals without needing to use a middle-man such as a bank or credit union. Because there are no bank fees or commissions, the loans available are often at lower than market rates.

Other methods of acquiring capital for your proposed business include things such as angel investors, convertible debt instruments, customer lenders, factoring and hedge-fund lenders. Credit cards are a means of generating quick cash, but they tend to be expensive and if you miss a payment or two the loan rate can go way up. We will leave this research up to you because as the years go by, other methods of financing a new business will be developed. We just wanted to let you know that you have alternatives to the major banks and credit unions when shopping for a loan.

Because we are using a retail shop as an example of a family business, here are a few things you should consider. Perhaps the biggest issue is where to locate your business. You want a location with good foot traffic. But that traffic should include customers who will be interested in what you are selling. The best way to find out if a location is appropriate is to give it a trial run. That can be a little difficult because the owners of business property often want a 5- to 10-year lease. Fortunately there is a way to test the waters before committing to a long-term lease. Storefront (http://www.thestorefront.com/) specializes in the rental of short-term "pop-up" retail spaces. The spaces can range from a few square feet of space in an existing retail shop to the entire store. The length of the rental can range from day-to-day up to a few months at a time.

Storefront.com's properties tend to be in larger cities and may not list a space in the community you are interested in. That's ok. You can take the initiative and approach business owners on your own to see if you can rent a small retail area from them. It is similar to someone renting out an extra bedroom in their house. Be sure to mention that your marketing campaign will bring more customers through their door and that they could see improved business from the increased traffic.

If your small shop is successful, then you can be more confident about signing a long-term lease in the area. If your results are not too good, it might be something other than the location. Your marketing might not be effective. These days a small business can reach far more people for free thanks to social media outlets. Create a Facebook Page then ask all the people on your various social networks to spread the word about your new business. We created our Facebook page following the suggestion we found in the blog post How to Create a Facebook Business Page-in 5 Simple Steps at blog.hubspot.com/. For other marketing ideas be sure to talk with the folks at your local Small Business Administration office and search Google for marketing concepts.

Find your local Small Business Development Center (SBDC) at – https://www.sba.gov/tools/local-assistance/sbdc. You can search this site's list by state. Your local SBDC office offers free business consulting. In addition SBDC offices provide low-cost training services including: business plan development, manufacturing assistance, financial packaging and lending assistance. Other services include exporting and importing support, disaster recovery assistance, procurement and contracting aid, market research help, 8(a) Business Development Program support, and healthcare guidance.

Family Investment and Overall Business Management

As discussed in Chapter 6, Children it is important to learn to manage money. We don't mean a personal budget so that you can take vacations; we mean management of family money for multiple generations (so that they can have vacations too). Topics include how much financial support is expected from family members, what the family investment portfolio might look like and the conduct and management of family businesses.

Families with substantial investments and businesses should look into some form of holding company. This allows for managing diverse assets while keeping the liability issues under control. In this section we deal with how family business holdings are managed – not the personal money and investments of individual family members. We would expect that individuals in your line family would be solely responsible for their own personal investments, property, money, etc. and that they would be separate from family holdings.

Note: We feel that family members should have their own personal money and property such as clothes or musical instruments. Even in a line family, people are individuals. Each member of your family should have their own money for personal items and entertainment such as going to movies, concerts or whatever.

Limited Liability Company

Now we are going to look at the limited liability company model (LLC). This is an excellent tool for both investing a pool of money and managing the investments for multiple generations. LLC money may be invested in all the investment instruments listed earlier and can be used for start-up businesses.

First a definition of what an LLC is and is not. It is not a corporation and, therefore, is not required to keep minutes or have a board of directors. However, if you are using the consensus procedure, notes are taken (and we feel that no matter the process, notes are a good idea). As with S-corporations, LLCs pay no income taxes. The income tax responsibility "flows through" the LLC to the individual members of the LLC thus avoiding what some call "double taxation."

Unlike a common partnership where profits are split 50/50, an LLC can have custom methods of profit distribution. Also LLC owners (members) have liability protection similar to the protection afforded to a corporation's board members and shareholders. Unless a member signs a personal guarantee, creditors cannot go after a member's personal assets.

LLCs are a powerful yet flexible management tool. LLC operating agreements can cover issues such as keeping family members from selling their shares of the LLC to people outside of the family. Without this option, you could have non-family members suddenly involved in the heart of family finances. LLC operating agreements can require family members to make contributions of cash or other negotiable instruments to the LLC on a regular basis. LLCs can stop managers from investing in certain types of businesses such as arms manufacturers or they can dictate that the LLC only invest in Laundromats in particular parishes or counties (we don't recommend limiting your LLC this radically).

Your LLC operating agreements can provide for the management style to be used – from rotating planning boards, majority voting, family consensus, etc. (See Chapter 7, Family Decision Making.) Check out your local laws, rules and requirements for LLCs because they differ from state to state. Apparently it is possible to form an LLC in a state other than where you live. However, an LLC cannot be invested in real estate in any state other than where it was formed. That means a Delaware LLC cannot have rental property in New York or any other state.

We have heard that the rules in Delaware and Nevada have advantages such as Delaware's low setup cost. If your family wants to start an LLC, study the subject and get professional legal help. All we have done is to tell you that this tool is available for your family's use.

General Partnership

A simple and cheap way to form a business with multiple owners is the general partnership. Each state has specific rules relating to general partnerships, but we are only going to go over some general topics that should apply to most localities.

When two or more people start a business enterprise as owners, they usually become members of a general partnership by default. A general partnership can be based on an oral agreement or even a simple handshake. We feel that it is best to get an agreement in writing. Each owner can agree to a specific percentage of the partnership. In turn, each owner is responsible for investing a defined amount of money. This could be a one-time payment, a monthly payment or any other type of investment strategy agreed to by all the partners.

Be aware that if one partner makes a contract or incurs a debt in the name of the partnership, all other partners are liable for that contract or debt. The term for this situation is "unlimited liability." You must trust the people with whom you establish a general partnership. Management of the general partnership is shared with all other partners. However, your agreement can assign specific management duties to a particular partner. Each partner of a general partnership has a duty to tell all the other partners about any information that affects the business. Partnership profits and losses are shared proportionally depending on the percentage of ownership each partner controls. In a line family, partnership agreements should probably have a buy-out clause in case one owner wishes to take their profits for use in some other project.

Family Investment Club

Members of your family can pool their money for investing thereby creating an investment club. As long as good records are kept this can be a powerful way for ordinary people to get into serious investing. An investment club is a for-profit business. The default legal entity of such a club is usually a general partnership (see above). However, your family investment club can use legal tools such as LLCs and various forms of incorporation to manage the club's resources. General partnerships usually require no formal operating agreement; however, we recommend that you look into the possibility of writing one. Other types of legal entities usually require an operating agreement.

Your investment club operating agreement must have details about its purpose and operation. As a starting point, you can use one or more of the many online sources for operating agreement templates and samples. These online resources are only a starting point. Gather your family members who want to be part of the investment club together to create a rough draft of an operating agreement. When you are finished, take the draft to your lawyer and let her or him check it over. You want this document to be complete and accurate. There are tax issues to be discussed when selecting the type of legal entity your investment club will become.

A Couple of Rules of the Rich

1. Multigenerational fortunes make money through business holdings and investments.
2. Wealthy families keep their money through the rule of thirds; one-third real estate, one-third gold and one-third fine art. We suggest starting with real estate.

Note: No financial instruments were bought, sold, harmed or recommended in the writing of this book.

We strive to provide accurate information and invite corrections from anyone with legal or other related professional credentials. Contact us through our website, http://www.line-family.info/.

Elon's Opinion on Finances

I hate talking about money! I always get emotional. It's embarrassing to admit, but I'm afraid it is true. It's probably some deep seated thing left over from childhood. Most of our "stuff" is. How well do you handle money and talks about money? I know that some of you are much better at handling money and financial conversations than I am. My suggestion for your line family is to find the people who are the best with money, including budgeting and investing, and give them the job of handling the finances, subject to review by other members of the family. It probably shouldn't be left to just one person, or to anyone for an overly long time. Even people who are interested in money matters, and are good at it, can burn out eventually. A strong core vision and strong intimate connections are crucial for a line family, but if your money issues are not well taken care of, it is likely that your family will not survive very long. However, I believe that the possibilities are really good for long-term financial success if your group takes the time and effort to learn to manage your resources well.

CHAPTER SIX

Children

It's always better to outnumber the children.

Richard Gilmore

We want to be clear – there is no need to have children in a line family. As with nuns and monks, who have continued their lines for centuries, a line family's future depends on bringing in new – and mostly younger – members. There are many fine methods of birth control available. Some methods are more reliable than others and some more permanent than others. Also there are new birth control methods being developed all the time. But let's be honest (or at least pragmatic) babies will probably happen.

How do You Define Parents?

How do parenting responsibilities work in a line family? You might choose to have the biological parents have all the responsibilities. This seems at odds with the line family model. It also seems at odds with human nature. Other family members, besides the birth parents, will love and cherish the children. It is easy to love a child not related by blood. If you don't think so, talk to adoptive parents about their love and dedication to their adopted children. With a line family you have created a village that, as an African proverb said, is needed to raise a child. Most people in your line family will be involved with the children.

We will not go much into strategies for raising children, their care, feeding or social training. There are many books written on those subjects. We do want to say however that children are resilient and adaptable. Maybe being in a line family will be difficult to explain to friends and teachers, but dealing with challenges is one of the many things people have to learn. From our experience in the poly community, we have seen many children thrive in multi-adult households. As long as children are loved and protected, the vast majority seems to do fine, though some complain that with so many adults caring for them they can't get away with anything.

Sometimes things go wrong. Here are some examples of stories that actually happened.

Incarceration

A 28-year-old Louisiana single mother of two was wrongly arrested by a Florida sheriff's office. The charge was felony theft. The woman had no prior felony arrest records and had never heard of, let alone visited, Clay County, Florida where the crime occurred.

The woman, a mother of a 2-year-old son and a 12-year-old daughter, said that the Florida sheriff's office was "ruining my life" and that the arrest had caused her to lose her home. There is at least one lady with the same first and last name as the accused woman who is also from Louisiana. A public defender that worked on the case said his office was able to produce medical records showing that the accused woman was in an Arkansas hospital at the time of the initial grand theft robbery for which she was wrongly arrested.

She was in jail for nearly four weeks. Then - while in a court hearing on the theft case - she was arrested again and booked back into the Clay County jail for another crime that had been committed by the woman with the same name. After spending another week in jail, she was released and finally the charges against her were dropped.

Death

A couple was killed in a violent wreck on a Friday around 2:30 a.m. The victims were a 37-year-old man and a 38-year-old woman. They were the parents of five children ages 1 to 13 years old. The wreck involved only their car. No evidence of drugs or alcohol was found. The vehicle was traveling on a highway with a posted speed limit of 55 mph. For some reason the vehicle crossed left of the center line and struck a culvert. Maybe the driver was drowsy; maybe they were avoiding a pet or other animal wandering on the road. The car went out of control and struck a utility pole before coming to rest upside down in a ditch.

Mental Illness

An estimated 26.2 percent of Americans ages 18 and older – about one in four adults – have a diagnosable mental disorder in any given year, according to National Institute of Mental Health statistics. (http://www. thekimfoundation.org/html/about_mental_ill/statistics.html). But what is mental illness? More research needs to be done, but many physical illnesses have documented psychiatric symptoms. Richard experienced major depression in his early life. To be clear, clinical depression is not being really sad about something. Depression can simply turn emotions off. The world – and the people in it – holds little interest to a person so afflicted.

Richard's cholesterol levels were extremely low as a child and young adult. His doctor described him as being in the lower one-half of one percentile of the US population for serum cholesterol. The majority of young people with cholesterol that low die from suicide or violent accident. Richard later found out that cholesterol is essential for the creation of a certain type of serotonin receptor that seems to inhibit self-destructive behavior.

http://www.psychologytoday.com/blog/evolutionary-psychiatry/201103/low-cholesterol-and-suicide

Our good friends at the American Bar Association have put together an excellent site called, Mental & Physical Ability in Custody Determinations. Check it out at: www.americanbar.org/content/dam/aba/migrated/domviol/pdfs/ability_in_custody.authcheckdam.pdf. The site has an alphabetical listing of states, references to their codes and statutes and a summary of the law. Montana is missing from this list for some reason.

Why have we told you all this? Because your children depend on you. They depend on you for food, affection, shelter and to be kept out of protective custody by the state. The above scenarios can happen to anyone through little or no fault of their own. In fact, all of the above stories did happen. You can have a say in your child's welfare in spite of death, incarceration or mental incapacity. If you are a legal parent, you need to consider drawing up a protection plan for your children.

Kids Protection Plan

We met Alexis M. Neely at a conference in Denver Colorado. She is a former attorney who was presenting a talk about legal issues for polyamorous families. Of all the issues she talked about, protecting children from being placed in state custody was the one she emphasized most. She believes so strongly in protecting children from the emotional trauma of being taken from their home that she has set up a website that will show you how to craft a child custody protection plan for free. If you are a parent, or know someone who is a parent, please visit her website at, http://kidsprotectionplan.com/.

We have to say that most foster homes have good people taking care of the children. However, in researching this issue, we found a not insignificant number of stories about foster homes where neglect and abuse were perpetrated against the children in their care. Even before a foster home is involved, think about the trauma a child experiences when a police officer shows up at the door and tells the babysitter (or a member of your line family) that the parents are in the hospital. Unless the caretaker can produce a signed child protection plan, the police officer has no choice but to take the children into custody. Police officers don't want to remove children from their homes, the children certainly don't want to leave with a stranger and the caretaker feels helpless. Do everyone a favor and look into writing a protection plan for your children. And make sure that anyone caring for your children has ready access to the document.

Birthrate Control

Following is a sample age demographic for a line family with 24 adults. Let's further assume a nearly equal gender distribution among the age groups. The age distribution might look like this:

Age Range	30s	40s	50s	60s	70s	80s	90s
# of People	3	5	6	4	3	2	1

Now let's stipulate that this line family has a commitment to a lower birthrate and strives for one live birth for every female of childbearing age. This family would have about 4 to 7 children under the age of 18, depending on when each woman chooses to have a child. Even at this smaller birthrate the children would have siblings. We have heard a surprising number of parents say that the main reason they have a second child is so that the first child won't be alone. This line of logic could be a rationalization or a real concern. Either way, a line family would most likely provide siblings from other family members. In addition, the children would have many adults to love and care for them.

Birthrate control, as described above, can have a significant positive effect on the family finances. Using the lower birthrate plan, the financial commitment of raising children is about half of what it would be if every man felt they needed to have genetic offspring. A dear, life-long friend – who is a molecular biologist – told us that, "There is nobody with DNA so special that the human race must have their genetic code passed along." What is important to the life of a child is the love they receive from the adults in their life as well as the examples set by those adults.

One member of our family has experienced parenting a couple of children that were not genetically related to them. That person shared the joys and tribulations of child rearing with the biological parents. Strong emotional bonds were created. People can experience the fulfillment and frustration of raising children even if they are not related by blood – it doesn't matter. Adoption is also a path to consider. We are not sure what an adoption agency would make of a line family, but it's worth a try. There are plenty of children that need homes – especially older children.

What do Children of Both WWII Veterans and the Wealthy Have in Common?

Returning veterans of WWII came home and found that they were to receive benefits from something called the GI Bill of Rights. It gave veterans full tuition benefits to attend college. In addition to tuition, text books and room and board were also fully paid as long as the veteran was attending school. The GI Bill also provided low-cost home loans. Many veterans thrived because of the GI bill and became successful businessmen.

We read about a researcher who had interviewed a roomful of businessmen who were also WWII vets. The interviewer asked for a show of hands of those who had taken advantage of the GI Bill. All but a couple of men raised their hands. The interviewer asked for those hands to remain raised if they had helped their children by paying for their schooling or buying them a starter home. Only a couple of hands went down. These veterans had learned the value of having an education that left them with no debts. This understanding of the value in getting a solid financial start in life and a good education meant that most of them helped their children in a similar manner. Their children benefitted from their father's valuable experience.

Wealthy families know this and provide their children with education and a strong financial start in life. Bill Gates said: "I will give the kids some money but not a meaningful percentage. Setting the number so that they need to work but they feel reasonably taken care of is hard to figure out." We are sure that his kids will also receive 1st class educations.

Warren Buffett had faced the issue of how much money to give his three children as they were starting out. Buffett said that it was his intention to give his kids, "enough money so they would feel they could do anything, but not so much that they could do nothing." And decades later they are all doing very well.

General tenants of good parenting still apply. Children of any social class need to be taught the values of responsibility and respect regarding the Earth, family, friends and all of life. The details we leave up to you; however, we do feel that children need to learn to manage and make money. We look to Warren Buffett again because he has developed a children's educational program called the, "Secret Millionnaires Club." As of June 2015 you can see episodes at the website, http://www.smckids.com/episodes/. Here you will find short animated stories of children learning about business basics, money management, basic investing, borrowing, etc. Each webisode is 3- to 4-minutes long. At present there are 26 webisodes waiting to entertain and inform your children about managing and making money. Bonus, Warren Buffett plays a part in each lesson. You should check it out just to see Buffett as a cartoon character.

Making money is not the same as managing money. Having one skill does not necessarily lead to the other. We are confident that Bill Gates' children will learn how to manage money before they receive any sizable sum. Of course Bill doesn't have to give a large lump sum to his kids. Let's look at how long-term wealthy families handle managing gifts of money.

Giving Children Money

Several ways are available to give children money for any reason. The most straight forward is a gift. Here's what the IRS website has to say about gifts.

Gift Tax: "The gift tax is a tax on the transfer of property by one individual to another while receiving nothing, or less than full value, in return. The tax applies whether the donor intends the transfer to be a gift or not.

The gift tax applies to the transfer by gift of any property. You make a gift if you give property (including money), or the use of or income from property, without expecting to receive something of at least equal value in return. If you sell something at less than its full value or if you make an interest-free or reduced-interest loan, you may be making a gift."

This is the IRS' own interpretation of the tax code as it stands in December 2014 (http://www.irs.gov/Businesses/Small-Businesses-&-Self-Employed/Gift-Tax).

Who Pays the Gift Tax?

The donor is generally responsible for paying the gift tax. Under special arrangements the person receiving the gift may agree to pay the tax instead. Please visit with your tax professional if you are considering this type of arrangement.

As of 2014, total gifts valued at $14,000 or less to a single person in a single year are not taxed. Not all gifts must be declared however, even if the total value exceeds $14,000 in a single year. Gifts for tuition are not taxed at any amount. Also gifts to pay medical expenses of an individual are not subject to the gift tax. Neither are gifts to a legal spouse or political organizations.

Instead of just handing a large check to a child, you might want to look at trusts for giving money to children. You can set up a trust to pay for tuition and books or to provide simple living expenses on a regular basis. The giver has more control over disbursement of funds with a trust. (See Chapter 5, Finances for more details.) For complete and up to date details go to the I.R.S. gift tax page (www.irs.gov/Businesses/Small-Businesses-&-Self-Employed/Frequently-Asked-Questions-on-Gift-Taxes). You can find all of the links mentioned in this book at www.line-family.info/CALF_companion. The links are arranged by chapter and in the order presented in the book.

529 College Savings Plan

You can save for a child's college education using a 529 plan. They are available in most states. The 529 college savings plan is named for Section 529 of the Internal Revenue code. Under this code you contribute after-tax money and your money grows tax-free. All withdrawals are tax-free when used for tuition, room and board, and other qualified higher education expenses. Check out more information and a list of states with 529 programs at www.sec.gov/investor/pubs/intro529.htm.

First Home

Buying a first home is more difficult than purchasing the next home. There are two main reasons. The first is lack of a credit history. Most people's credit history starts with paying utility- and consumer-credit bills while renting a place to live. The second and bigger reason is lack of a down payment. A young person's income is generally fairly modest. This usually makes saving money for a down payment difficult.

If your line family has the wherewithal, you might want to think about buying a child's first home outright and then selling it to the child for a reduced price at a minimum interest rate. This way they learn about making regular payments. This mimics the GI Bill's inexpensive home loan program. Or you might give the home outright to the child. The gift of a home would probably generate a gift tax. But then, even the reduced price or lower than market interest loan might also be considered a gift.

Imagine what your life would have been like if you had started out on a solid financial footing with an excellent education and no burdensome debt. That's how the wealthy families do it. They give their children financial security to get going in life. Of course the children of the wealthy also have the advantage of readymade contacts which have been established by their family. Contacts are a type of capital that would be beneficial for your line family to cultivate.

Just know that your children will make mistakes. That is one reason why large lump sums of money may not be the best thing for adolescents or young adults. Ideally people need to know how to manage money before they acquire it. Trust accounts can be used to spread out the early financial support. These are things that your family might want to plan for in advance.

Hopefully that wise child, now an adult, that your line family raised and launched into the world will start (or find) their own line family. Of course you hope that other families have raised equally wise children who will eventually find their way into your family.

Elon's Opinion on Children

I chose not to have children. Have I regretted that? Not as much as I have missed having grandchildren. In a line family, I could have the same experience as having grandchildren - kids that I could spend time with when I wanted to and then send them to their parents. Selfish? Maybe. I won't go into my reasons for deciding to not have children, other than to say that it started with my decision to divorce my first husband. If we had been part of a line family, we might not have separated. And I might even have chosen to have a child. But I digress.

In the early drafts of this book we didn't include much about children. As we gathered information, we found that there was a lot that we had not thought about concerning what happens to kids if their parents die, become seriously ill, or are otherwise unable to care for them. I believe that the advice about creating a signed child protection plan is one of the most valuable pieces of information in this book for anyone who has the primary responsibility for a child's welfare.

One of my favorite things about the line family structure is that it can help to create a secure future for the children of the family and for the adults as they age. There isn't much of that left in our society of nuclear families, other than for the wealthiest families - that are often structured much like a line family.

CHAPTER SEVEN

Family Decision Making

> *If war is the violent resolution of conflict, then peace*
> *is not the absence of conflict, but rather, the ability to*
> *resolve conflict without violence.*

C.T. Butler

Family Decision-Making Techniques

What is your favorite color? Why would your answer to this question cause family fights, divorce, political upheaval or civil war? Your favorite color is an insignificant issue… isn't it? Maybe.

Try substituting political party, political system or economic system for color. How would that question change in importance if we were talking about race relations or nationalities? If you substitute religion for color in that question, it is possible that all hell will break loose. To better understand the dynamics of these conflicts, let's take it back to the simple question of favorite color.

For the sake of discussion we'll say that a couple is talking about the base color to paint the living room walls. Carol wants a blue theme, but Ted thinks a warmer approach is best and lobbies for orange. Carol's favorite color is a light tint of blue while Ted's favorite color is a darker shade of orange. Who's right? Please gentle reader, do not involve your favorite color when deciding this issue. Whose truth is correct?

Did you decide Carol is right and Ted has no design sense, or did you decide the other way around? In deciding one way or another, you make one person right and one person wrong. Imagine how many people would be wrong if this were a foursome and Bob and Alice had other ideas. Suddenly you have as many as three people who are wrong. Not a happy situation.

Take a moment to consider that both Carol and Ted are right. Carol's favorite color is a light blue while Ted's favorite color is dark orange. There is no conflict because their favorite color statements are true for Carol and Ted even though the colors are different. In this case we are dealing with truths. Truth is relative. Truths can change. Ted used to have hunter green as a favorite color. Who knows what caused it to change. Does it really matter? His favorite color truth has changed over the years. Truth is subjective.

By contrast, let's look at some facts. The wavelength interval of orange is 590 to 635 nanometers while the frequency interval is 480 to 510 Tera hertz. For blue the wavelength interval is 450 to 490 nanometers and the frequency interval is 610 to 670 Tera hertz. Whether you love or hate orange or blue, these facts remain the same and are measurable and provable. Facts are objective.

It is the subjective and non-provable things that we disagree about, fight about and defend against the heathens and barbarians who hold different views. When we hold truths to be absolute and applicable to everyone in every situation, we run afoul of others who hold contradictory truths to be absolute and also applicable to all. So how does a line family full of intelligent people go about choosing the color scheme for the common rooms?

Maybe you get lucky and everyone who has an opinion agrees

without much discussion. Some might see this as a result of the process of consensus – but it wasn't. You were lucky enough to have a 100% perfect majority. Now, what color scheme for the building's exterior walls and trim? We can pretty much guarantee you won't get a perfect majority on this topic. Some people will have little interest in what the colors will be. Others will be quite opinionated on the subject. What's a civilized line family to do?

You have options in the decision-making process. We will look at these processes and their pros and cons. Group decision-making tools take many forms for many types of groups such as engineering design teams, business managers and presidential cabinets. Many tools are specifically designed for these specialty groups. If your family businesses grow large enough, you may want to study this topic further. There's lots of information online. Remember that your family does not have to pick one method for decision making and use it exclusively. We feel that each option has its place.

We will stick to more general techniques that a family can use in the management of family property and other day to day issues. All of these techniques fall under one of four categories, unilateral action by an individual, plurality (agreement of the largest group even if they don't hold a majority), majority agreement (aka the tyranny of the 51%) and unanimous agreement (a tough standard).

———————————

The methods we will be discussing are:

Majority Rule	Expert Opinion
Brainstorming	Nominal Group Technique
Dot Voting	Individual Initiative
Idea Rating Sheets	Voting Credits
Rotating Planning Board	Formal Consensus
Dialectical Inquiry	Loomio Online Tool

Majority Rule

Who hasn't used this? We find majority rule voting in elementary school classes, groups of friends and occasionally in selecting the President of the United States. For a small group it's a quick way to make choices. Quickness is its major advantage. Majority rule voting does have its place. If the question being voted on is of limited consequence, it might be the way to go. For example, what movie is going to be shown in the family theater on the big screen? Those who lose out on this vote can perhaps watch another movie on another TV or their computer, tablet or phone.

Otherwise a non-binding vote can be used to see how the group stands on an issue. In the best case, it is a shortcut to resolutions. Otherwise it could indicate how much work is needed to find a solution to a question. In the worst case the process can involve adversarial debate and the formation of competing factions.

A Unanimous Vote for Eviction

In 2008 the Lahar Creek Creative Community purchased 27 acres of land in the foothills of the Cascade Mountains. The property included a barn and two small cabins. It was a short sale and the community LLC got it for an excellent price. The new property was almost totally paid for by the sale of a smaller community property in a more expensive, suburban location.

Community members wanted to use the two cabins for art studios. Fortunately Ned, who had been in the Army, had found a couple of surplus army Jamesway huts. He convinced the community to buy them because they would provide immediate shelter on any property they would buy. A Jamesway hut is an insulated tent that closely resembles a Quonset hut. It has a 16' by 32' floor and was specifically designed for arctic conditions. The hut includes a flue so that a small wood stove or other heater can be used. One hut was used for storage and the other hut was used as a temporary dormitory for the initial 8 residents.

One of the cabins became the kitchen and dining hall. Community weekly meetings were to be held in the other cabin. There was just one little problem. It seems the previous owners had a couple of dogs. Unlike most rural folks, these previous owners let their two large dogs go freely in and out of this cabin and sleep in the cabin at night. When the dogs departed with their owners, they left their fleas behind. Now the fleas were attending the first community meeting. It ended up being one of the shortest meetings they ever held. They made only one resolution – evict the fleas – the vote was a unanimous voice vote.

Back at the dining hall they also voted unanimously to use natural methods to kill the fleas. They chose techniques that would not leave residual poisons that would harm people, animals or plants. To isolate the problem they flame torched the earth around the cabin then applied diatomaceous earth. In the cabin they tried homemade sprays consisting of a mixture of vinegar, lemon juice and Witch hazel. They tried dry salt and boric acid all over the floor followed by vacuuming. Then they tried Rosemary and Peppermint. Nothing worked. They finally tried a chemical bomb. That seemed to work for about a week, and then the fleas were back.

Patty, the founder of the community, picks up the story from here. "I remembered back at the first weekly meeting that I first saw the fleas on Lisa. She was wearing white socks. It was scary how quickly they jumped on her. I had a cat as a child, so I knew about using a flea comb and drowning the fleas I caught in a bowl of soapy water. I eventually put those two things together and came up with a plan.

I announced that we were resuming our meetings in the flea infested cabin. I told everyone to wear cutoffs and knee-high white socks. Everyone would also bring a bucket, bowl or some such container of soapy water. We all picked fleas off our socks and dropped them in soapy water as we sat in a circle discussing community business. Some folks got a little competitive about it. Our first meeting back in the cabin was not very productive from a business sense. Most of the people were trying to keep track of the number of fleas they were picking off their socks. I said that if people wanted to compete, they could come back on their own time and have flea killing contests, but we needed to get community business done.

I think Barney claimed to have killed the most fleas in a single meeting. Most people didn't want to try counting dead flea bodies floating in soapy water. After a little over three months of flea-murdering business meetings we finally had a meeting without fleas. Most of us still dress for our business meetings in shorts and white knee-highs. It's kind of a tradition now. It reminds us that as a community we can solve tough problems."

———————————

We do believe that majority rule voting has one critical use… admission of a new member. Our guess is that a vote for a new line family member must be 100 percent "yes". Consensus can be used, but we feel that little discussion should be needed because any potential member should already be well known to every member of the family. This would be accomplished by whatever family rule you have for vetting prospective members. Some of those rules might include living with the family for a year, spending a minimum amount of time with each member of the family and/or getting involved in a family business or project. Everyone should have a good feeling about the person before the vote. Family members should also feel comfortable talking with each other about the potential member during any trial period. Hopefully the vote will be a formality.

Brainstorming

Brainstorming usually has little structure to it. However it is more than just a few family members sitting around drinking beer and proposing "what if" senarios. That is called a "bull session." We're not saying that great ideas can't come from such informal gatherings, but choices made affecting family resources must have some form of record keeping about the topics opened for consideration. Otherwise the ideas put forward are about as valuable as that great idea that occurred to you while sleeping that you can't remember in the morning.

It is preferable to have the whole family at the brainstorming session. A facilitator needs to be appointed. Next the perceived problem must be described in enough detail so that group members have a good understanding of the issue to be discussed. The facilitator asks for ideas from all members of the family. The facilitator, or someone appointed as secretary, records the ideas presented. Use a paper flip chart, white board or other device that is easily visible to everyone. In the case of temporary displays such as a white board or chalk board, take photos before the information is erased.

As ideas are proposed and recorded, family members are not allowed to comment, groan, applaud, roll their eyes, cheer or make any other gesture that would make it uncomfortable for subsequent group members to propose ideas. After all family members have had a chance to get their ideas recorded the evaluation process can begin. Each idea is discussed in turn without generalized negative comments. Discussion should focus on topics such as cost, functionality, duration, scalability, etc.

Online brainstorming is also possible. It provides two main advantages. The first is that family members do not have all to be in the same room at the same time. It can be quite difficult to get a dozen or more people together as vacation schedules vary, business trips can happen on short notice and occasionally people do get sick.

The second benefit of online brainstorming is the ability of shy people to post ideas anonymously. Not every poly person is an extrovert. But introverts can be extremely creative.

Dot Voting

Richard was part of a social organization that had monthly events for the local poly community. Richard explains, "Once a year our organization held a planning meeting during the first hour or so of our regular social gathering. Our job was to come up with ideas for the following year's activities. It was the organizer's attempt to plan party themes and events that would not bomb. You might think a retrospective movie night of political propaganda films from the first half of the 20th century would be a big draw, but you never know. Sometimes the planning meeting would 'bomb' and people would show up an hour late to avoid the planning session as the second half of the night was devoted to dancing and snacking on goodies that people brought to put on the refreshment table.

One of the organizers, Shelly (not her real name) came up with a new idea for the planning meetings. She showed up with peel-and-stick dots. They were large (1") blue dots and small (1/2") green dots. Everyone was given 5 blue and 20 green dots. We were told that these were our votes. The blue dots represented activities we 'desperately' wanted to attend and the green dots indicated activities we would probably attend. A person could put all of their blue and green dots on one event idea if they felt the need; however, we were encouraged to spread them around on several ideas we liked or were at least likely to attend.

Shelly had already written on individual pieces of paper many of the more popular events we had done in the past. A couple of the old events were voted down by the group and removed from consideration. Next the group considered new ideas. These ideas were each given their own pieces of paper. I had done a karaoke show in the past and it was already up for consideration, however the propaganda film night was nowhere to be seen.

All of the event idea papers were taped to the wall. During the rest of the evening, people put their dots on the ideas they liked. Some people voted early, others voted later. Various reasons were given. The early voters thought that their votes might sway the later votes. People who took longer to vote generally said that they wanted to really consider the options. It also gave them a chance to talk about the ideas they supported and try to gain the support of people who still had dots. I voted late to see how my karaoke show was doing without any influence from me. I was happy to see that the karaoke show was popular. I did put one of my large blue dots on the karaoke event. I like doing the show, but I used the rest of my dots to vote for other events.

As the evening went on I noticed that a few people had dots stuck to their foreheads or on their clothing. None of the people sporting dots would say what kind of event they represented. A couple of them blushed when I asked. This was very funny as I rarely see poly people blushing. Shelly had two large blue dots on her clothing by the end of the evening. I feel that this represented the laid-back attitude around the voting process. Everyone had more than one vote and didn't feel the pressure of having to select only one idea. It is a pretty 'poly' way of making your opinions known. As the saying goes, you can love more than one. You can like blues dancing and karaoke. Why should you have to choose one or the other? (In case you are wondering, my karaoke show and a blues dancing class both were voted as events for the coming year.) Dot voting has turned the planning meeting into a relaxed and even fun event and improved participation in the process."

In the next section we will look at Idea Rating Sheets. This technique captures more detailed information, for example, whether someone disagrees or is neutral on a subject. If someone is neutral about a social event, they probably will not attend. Also people who are not interested or actively despise an event will not show up. In dot voting we are only concerned with the apparent popularity of an event idea. Not voting for an event captures the "I'm not coming" vote. Whether a person hates an idea or is just not interested, the result is the same. Therefore, dot voting seems to be an excellent choice for this situation. Also we like the positive vibe of voting for what you like.

Idea Rating Sheets
(Formerly known as Dotmocracy)

You can find Idea Rating Sheets online at the following website, http://www.idearatingsheets.org/. They seem a little sensitive about Dot Voting because people used to confuse it with their former name, Dotmocracy. The name Idea Rating Sheets is a much better choice except for its acronym, IRS.

How Idea Rating Sheets are used: A meeting is called and an open-ended question is asked to get people thinking about a topic. Open-ended questions are things like, where should we go on our vacation? Discussions of the question are held by the group as a whole or in smaller groups. After some set period of time, idea rating sheets are passed out. People then write ideas or comments about the question in section A of the form (see the following illustration). A person can use several forms if they have more than one comment or idea about the question.

Next, all the forms with ideas or comments are placed on a table or tables so that everyone can move around and read all the comments. People can indicate how strongly they agree or disagree with the idea by coloring in a circle under the appropriate area in section B. If a person is so inclined, they can write a brief note about the reason for their vote in the lower half of the form. Finally, a signature is included on the right side of the page. If everything goes as planned, the number of filled in circles will match the number of signatures on each rating sheet.

A team of people then tally the results and make notes about the optional comments recorded in section C. Depending on the size of the meeting, this process could take a while. It seems like a statistical graphing program would be a useful tool for this task. However this can be done by hand. What the users of this technique hope for is a pattern that suggests the group's favorite ideas about the original question. If a lot of agreement is found in the forms, the group can act. If a trend is noticed, a new open-ended question can be asked at the next meeting that focuses on the trend.

Write one _idea_ here in large letters:						Signatures
A						D

Do you agree? **B** Fill your one dot below & sign on the right					
🙂 Strong Agreement	🙂 Agreement	😐 Neutral	🙁 Disagreement	☹ Strong Disagreement	❓ Confusion
OOOOOOOOOO OOOOOOOOOO OOOOOOOOOO	OOOOOOOOOO OOOOOOOOOO OOOOOOOOOO	OOOOOOOOOO OOOOOOOOOO OOOOOOOOOO	OOOOOOOOOO OOOOOOOOOO OOOOOOOOOO	OOOOOOOOOO OOOOOOOOOO OOOOOOOOOO	OOOOOOOOOO OOOOOOOOOO OOOOOOOOOO
Strengths & Opportunities C			**Concerns & Weaknesses** C		

Idea Rating Sheet Sections:

A. Where a person writes their idea about the question. It should be a single idea that is clearly described without the use of jargon or undefined acronyms.

B. People respond to the idea in this section. This is where you choose your level of enthusiasm for the idea or select "confusion" if you are not sure. You indicate your response by filling in one blank dot under your selection.

C. This section is optional. It allows you to give a brief statement about the reason for your rating of the idea.

D. Is for your signature. You may only fill in one dot on the form. When the procedure is finished, there must be the same amount of dots as there are signatures. This keeps people from cheating. We question the need for section D in a line family. You should be able to trust your fellow family members to fill in only one dot without needing to make them sign for it.

Idea Rating Sheets capture more information than the blue and green stickers used for dot voting. In addition to agreeing or strongly agreeing with a proposition, these forms also record if people are neutral, do not agree, strongly oppose or are confused regarding the idea. This system is too comprehensive for planning a monthly social event. It is excellent however for determining what negative issues people have with an established or proposed course of action.

Rotating Planning Board

Twin Oaks has used this method for decades. Their planning board consists of three people who are given staggered, 18-month terms. Every 6 months a new member joins the board as an existing member's term ends. Planning board members are temporary executives. At Twin Oaks a proposed member of the planning board can be blocked by a membership minority of 20% voting against them. Planning board decisions can be overruled by a simple majority of the membership (no dictatorial powers here). Members are encouraged to have private conversations with board members, write opinion papers and take polls to influence the board's actions. Weekly community meetings are also held with the board to further discuss community issues.

Twin Oaks' success speaks well to this kind of rotating management. It has worked for Twin Oaks for most of its history. And their history stretches back to 1967. In addition they have several businesses with associated managers and team members. Twin Oaks' population is generally around 100 including children. Your line family will probably not be that large. Though we suppose it is not out of the question to have 2 or 3 line families in some kind of intentional community relationship.

Dialectical Inquiry

We are not going to talk much about dialectical inquiry because of its adversarial nature; however, this technique does have the effect of breaking through groupthink behaviors. We want you to know its basics so that your family can make informed choices about this decision-making technique.

Debate is at the core of dialectical inquiry. There are two main ways to go about the procedure. One divides the group up as opposing camps. One group focuses on the positive attributes of a proposal. The other group looks for all the negative ramifications present in the idea. After a predetermined time for study and preparation, a debate is held. The debate outcome decides the fate of the issue at hand.

The second version of dialectical inquiry uses a single person representing the opposition to the proposal. Some call this using a "devil's advocate." It puts all the responsibility of researching and presenting the downside of an idea on a single person. While some people might enjoy this role, it seems to us that having more people considering an issue from all sides would yield better results.

Expert Opinion

A family would be wise to use its human capital when making choices about technical or professional issues. If your line family includes a lawyer, nurse, electrician, etc. it would be foolish to not give weight to their expertise when applicable. If the question before you is a matter of contracts, real-estate or tax laws, it would only make sense to give more weight to a lawyer's opinion. However, other individuals may have specific information that the subject matter expert does not have.

As an example: Richard learned from a yearly physical that his serum cholesterol was not within a range considered normal. The bloodwork report showed that his cholesterol level was extremely low – in the lower ½ of 1 percentile of the U.S. population. The doctor thought this was nothing but good news. Richard, however, felt it might not be a totally good thing. Cholesterol must be used for something or why would a human body store it?

He did some literature research at the local University's medical library (this was a few years before the "Internets"). He discovered the cholesterol molecule is a component of bile salts used for digestion. Cholesterol also gives cells membranes stiffness and stability. The body uses cholesterol in the repair of damaged blood vessels. Cholesterol is also needed for proper function of serotonin receptors in the brain. Low cholesterol levels had recently been linked to depression and suicidal tendencies. This was long before serotonin had become big news in the general media.

Richard presented his physician with the collected information. His doctor admitted that he was not aware of that recent line of research. For this specific and limited subject the patient was the medical knowledge expert because he had done the research and collected the data for presentation.

It is unreasonable to expect a professional in any field to know absolutely everything about their subject. Therefore, it is not advisable to give your subject matter expert total control over a decision in their field of expertise. However, individuals who bring up positions contrary to a professional's judgment will need to provide documentation to back up their objections or modification suggestions.

A Community Twice Blessed

Everyone at the Silent Beach intentional community agreed that they needed a new stove in the communal kitchen. Being a major purchase, a full membership meeting was called. Betty, the current meetings facilitator explains what happened next.

"Getting 25 adults to attend a meeting at the same time would be impossible if Skype did not exist. Two of our members were out of town. That wasn't too bad. Once, about a year ago, we had 9 members attend a meeting through Skype. We call it 'Skyping in.'

First I asked if anyone in the group felt that we didn't need to purchase a new stove. No one raised an objection. Next we needed to select our decision-making process. We often use consensus, but Barney raised his hand and asked to have expert knowledge privilege. That means he would be in charge of the selection of the stove – subject to final approval of the community members. Barney has been a professional cook on and off for over a dozen years. He worked in smaller family restaurants and cafes. Nothing fancy, but he knows his way around a kitchen and knows how to cook for a crowd. He does most of our communal meals. It was pretty easy to grant him expert status.

Barney stated his intention to purchase a professional grade, 36" gas stove with 6 burners. He said that the greater expense of a professional stove would actually be cheaper in the long run. A professional stove with less intense use than in a restaurant could last decades instead of just a few years for a residential model. Twenty-five people can age a residential appliance pretty quickly.

Wilma spoke up and said she had concerns about air quality. She also mentioned the problem of overheating the building in the summer. Wilma was an architectural student in her 3rd year. She was extremely interested in conservation techniques. For example, after she finished sealing the main building for excessive air leaks, our use of heating energy dropped by nearly a third.

She said that if we got the kind of stove Barney was talking about, that we would also needed to get a professional ventilation hood that moved at least 900 cubic feet of air per minute. Also there would have to be a source of make-up air to replace the hot, greasy, moist air being removed by the range hood. After much discussion it was decided that Wilma should have expert status as well. We had never before had more than one expert at a time on a project, but Barney agreed to Wilma's nomination."

Betty dismissed the meeting after scheduling a review meeting to take place 3 weeks later. They would review Barney and Wilma's suggestions. We asked how the review meeting went.

Betty said, "It was a smaller meeting because several people gave their proxy to Barney and Wilma. That means that they either trusted Barney and Wilma to make good choices or that they didn't do much cooking. As a result our review meeting attendance was 17.

Barney told us how he arrived at his decision. He had reviewed stoves based on features, user's reviews and price. Barney's first goal was a reliable machine with low maintenance. His second priority was price.

Wilma then described her ventilation system. Sometimes we're not sure if Wilma is going to be an architect or an engineer. She started to describe – in technical terms – how much of a thermal load the new stove would add to the kitchen and surrounding spaces like the dining hall, pantry and bathrooms. I had to interrupt her as I had noticed several people were getting that glazed over look in their eyes. I asked Wilma to focus on her conclusions and give us more 'bottom line' information."

Betty sat back and thought for a moment before concluding, "Giving two people expert privilege worked this time. I think that is because Barney and Wilma had respect for each other's expertise. Also they had no real reason for conflict because they were working on different parts of the project. I don't know what would have happened if we had two professional cooks. The process may not have gone so smoothly in that case."

We think that Betty's story shows that you can be flexible in how you use any decision-making technique. We had never considered a situation where there would be two knowledge experts working on an issue. So keep in mind that while there are several group decision-making techniques, each one can be modified to fit your family's situation. Please let us know what you come up with.

Nominal Group Technique

Nominal Group Technique (NGT) is similar to brainstorming but a bit more structured. As with brainstorming, NGT is readily adaptable to online use. It is designed to give family members time to carefully prepare their ideas in private. The time for preparation can vary from a few hours to a few days. Each person brings their written list of ideas to the meeting.

At the formal meeting a facilitator calls on people in turn. As people are called they present one of their ideas. A person can present multiple ideas, but only one is presented per turn. This continues around the room until all ideas are offered. Only questions for clarification are allowed at this time. During this process the information is recorded on paper or electronically. If electronic recording is used, there must be a projected image that everyone can see.

Now the group goes through the list of ideas discussing the pros and cons. Each idea is given a rating indicating its popularity. You can use stars, numbers, letters, etc. We suggest you avoid using classifications such as genius, idiotic, mundane, sublime…. Alienating your family members is not the goal of this technique. Reconsider the two or three top rated ideas to attempt to come to an agreement.

Individual Initiative

Situations can arise that call for immediate consideration by an individual family member. It's hard to believe that in a world of cell phones, wi-fi and the occasional pager that anyone is ever out of touch with anyone. But cell batteries die, cell coverage fails and coffee shops with free wi-fi occasionally close – and there you are with a killer deal on two full-cords of wood. Or maybe you found the perfect truck for a fair price with overload springs and a diesel engine that will run on peanut oil. These items have several folks interested and on the way, but you are there and have a family account checkbook.

Should the family allow for individual initiative so as not to miss the great deal or purchase of an item for which the family has been searching for a year and a half? What process should you have in place to review such individual actions? If an individual makes a poor choice, what should be the repercussions? Restricting the individual from making initiative purchases? Something more drastic, or a big hug and saying "nice try"? Does your family want to allow individual initiative purchases at all? Your family might want to discuss this possibility in advance.

To be clear, the individual initiative talked about in this section is based on a previous decision made by the family as a whole. In the above example of the purchase of a truck, we assume that the family had used some decision-making process to come to the conclusion that a truck of this type was needed. A vehicle is a large purchase and individual initiative should be used cautiously. Purchasing a cord of wood is a much smaller financial judgment and the consequences are not so far reaching. Still, the family's need for cordwood must exist before spending family money.

Voting Credits

We believe that important family decisions require more negotiation than a quick majority vote usually allows. Voting Credits encourage deliberation and puts something at stake for each family member. Our suggestion is that this system not be used for admitting new members to the family (see Majority Rule).

The Mechanics:
When a new member is added to the line family, they are given 500 credits (the number is just a suggestion). Having some credits gives the new member some voice in this system.

Ten credits/day are given to all family members. The longer you are in the family, the more credits you can accumulate - up to a limit. For this example we will use 10,000 credits as the limit. From a purely mathematical perspective, it would take just under 3 years to collect 10,000 voting credits. But in the real world, issues come up that need to be decided. And getting to 10,000 credits should not be a goal, at least not in our opinion. It is unlikely that many will reach the limit, and if they do it might be wise to have a conversation with them. Perhaps they, and the family as a whole, would benefit from them taking more interest in the family decision-making process.

In any issue to be decided by this system you may use up to 20% of the credits in your voting credit account. If a family member has somehow amassed the maximum 10,000 credits, it means he or she can put up to 2,000 credits into the voting. Using the maximum allowed voting credits means she or he is "all in." This is a powerful position to take and should not be done unless you are extremely passionate about the outcome.

The result of your 2,000 credit vote is that you now have only 8,000 credits. If there were a second issue on the table that day, your maximum number of available credits for voting would be 1,600 (20% of 8,000). The more a person throws their weight around, the lighter they become – quickly.

Feel free to use different numbers and percentages. This has just been an example. If you want to learn more, check out the website of the folks who developed this system (http://conceivia.com/).

Reasons to Use Voting Credits:

1. It captures the relative importance each member brings to an issue. For example, maybe you're a bicyclist and have little interest in the type of motor vehicle being purchased. You can use few or no credits to influence the result.

2. It tames people with control issues. It's true – there are folks

who try to get their own way on all issues. Using this voting system a person cannot dominate every issue that is brought before the family.

3. It allows for people with strong feelings about a particular issue to demonstrate how important it is to them.

Note: Your family should take notice if someone who normally has an even temperament when working on family issues suddenly goes "all in" to buck the trend of the talk. Pay close attention to what this family member is trying to say especially if it doesn't make sense to you when you first hear it.

The Conceivia website says it best, "Most people thought the air plane was a bad idea, and most new inventions for that matter. Almost all good ideas are considered bad ideas by the majority. We therefore can't rely on the majority to make decisions. We must make it possible for the individual to create. We must make it possible for a visionary to create a vision."

We don't think that the majority is always wrong, but the Conceivia website does make an interesting case. A good question to always ask yourself about a new or strange idea is, "Why not?"

4. The system encourages negotiation. You choose how many votes to risk. Voting credits are lost only if there is resistance to your proposition. Negotiating an agreement before voting saves everyone's credits. Talk to other family members, make compromises, listen to concerns, incorporate other's ideas if possible and iron out disagreements.

5. It reduces the formation of voting blocks, though it doesn't eliminate them.

Reasons Not to Use Voting Credits:

1. Someone has to be the system accountant.
Note: The folks who run the Conceivia site do not seem to understand the limited scalability of this system. We don't think that voting credits would work for a million people. However, for two or three dozen people we think it is a totally workable system.

A Decision to Ask People to Leave the Community

Over the years the Wayward Cooperative has added several members using a system of consecutive trial - and probationary - membership periods that generally last a total of two years. This lengthy process has produced good results in making sure that people fully experience what life is like in the community. (Note: Wayward is not a co-operative housing group. They just liked the term.) However, John told us a story that proves even the best systems can occasionally produce suboptimal results.

"A young couple with a young child came to live at the Wayward Cooperative. The couple seemed to have skills that would be of value to the community. Jaylin was a carpenter and Emory was an electrician. At least those were the skills they claimed – and used on a couple of small projects. They were accepted on a trial basis. After a year Emory and Jaylin applied for membership. They were accepted as probationary members. A probationary membership lasts for a year. During the probationary period things changed. In the first year they were productive people who participated in the community and were involved in community projects.

In the probationary year they became 'pot-heads' just hanging out and not involved with the community. They became needy using their child as an excuse. They asked for more and more help with the baby. They stopped doing any work for the community because of the baby. Some members gave them lots of support. Others started to judge Jaylin and Emory as not very knowledgeable or skillful parents.

We didn't anticipate that they would become so dependent. Emory and Jaylin's attitudes and behaviors became disruptive to the community. They were asked to leave. This was a real problem for the child and several of the community adults who had formed a relationship with the child. Many tears were shed."

John has noticed that when someone is asked to leave the community, the person being asked to leave does not want to believe that it was a collective decision. They tend to blame one person (usually one of the founders) for their expulsion. People seem to want to think they are being excluded because some individual with clout doesn't like them. It is probably easier to believe that just one person wants you gone rather than thinking several people want you to leave. John has a technique on how to avoid the single-person blame game.

"The pronouncement that someone needs to leave needs to be done collectively in a meeting, not privately by one person. This needs to be done in a special community meeting that makes the statement that we are collectively of the opinion that an individual (or couple) is not working out as a potential community member.

Sounds like a good idea, doesn't it? Since our experience with Jaylin and Emory, we have had to ask a couple of other trial members to leave. Even after going through the community meeting process, one individual blamed me for his expulsion. Amy later got blamed for being the one who got a woman expelled during her trial membership. The irony was that Amy was going to bat for her in the meeting where it was decided that she needed to go."

Problems will happen and mistakes will get made no matter how fair and reasoned your family's processes might be; no matter how carefully you plan for every eventuality. The best your family can do is to treat everyone with respect. It won't always be easy, few worthwhile things are.

Formal Consensus:

A detailed discussion of the formal consensus process is not possible for this book – this is only an introduction.

Consensus is a family decision-making process that calls for participation by everyone. The process assumes that each person's contribution is valuable. It encourages active listening by everyone to every person when they are sharing. It is one way that family members can get to know each other better. Respect for all voices is one of the fundamentals of consensus. Consensus allows us to practice a better way of dealing with each other. Also there are people who might never be heard if it were not for consensus.

Consensus also avoids the disenfranchisement and dissatisfaction of the minority. If people feel that they are having a decision forced on them they are likely to complain and cause discord in the family. People can consciously or unconsciously sabotage decisions in small or large ways, all because they don't feel their objections are really being heard. Most proposals can be modified until they are at least acceptable to most and tolerable to the rest.

Consensus has no winners or losers. One or more individuals put forward a proposal that involves or affects the family. Their proposal is open for all to comment on and share their concerns, suggest modifications or simply say nothing. The goal is to arrive at an outcome that all can share at some level. Everyone should feel that their concerns and suggestions, if any, have been resolved in some way.

In Consensus Everyone is Heard

You have probably been involved in informal consensus. For example, you are out with two or three good friends for dinner and a movie. Generally you will all have different ideas about what movie to see. Do you drag a good friend to a musical if you know that he hates musicals? Or do you find a film that you can all agree to see? The point is to spend time with friends, not see exactly what you want to see. So you compromise on a silly comedy, which you're just OK with attending. After all, you're good friends and you can bust his chops about his taste in films later.

Consensus takes time and can be hard work. Voting is simple and quick. Then, of course, a dictatorship is the most efficient form of government. Frankly we are more than a little suspicious of people who really want (or need) to be in charge of everything all the time.

Consensus Meeting Procedure Outline

1. Assemble at the agreed time and location.
2. Breathe together.
3. Declare safe space.
4. Check in.
5. Choose and/or introduce facilitator(s), note taker, mood monitor, optional peacekeeper and timekeeper.
6. Review the agenda or call for agenda items (proposals), establish priorities, set times for each item.
7. Read a proposal.
8. Take breaks, call for rounds (a discussion of a detail), check periodically to see how everyone is feeling.
9. Query for consensus.
10. Repeat steps 8 and 9 as needed.
11. Evaluate the meeting.
12. Close.

Deconstructing the Consensus Process

The family assembles at a predetermined time and location.

Get comfortable as a group. This could be as simple as everyone taking a few breaths together.

Declare and establish the meeting as a safe and respectful space (cast a protective circle if that is your tradition). Minimize distractions by turning off cell phones, computers, TVs, anything that beeps or otherwise draws attention.

Have everyone "check-in," and say how they are feeling at that moment. We feel that "being in the moment" is particularly important in this process.

Facilitator

Appoint a facilitator and optionally co-facilitator(s). Co-facilitators should trade off during the process, especially if one facilitator wants to express their concerns or propose modifications about the topic at hand. Otherwise the facilitator must strive to be neutral about the issue being discussed. The facilitator's main concern is making sure that everyone in the room feels heard by getting their ideas fully expressed. Optimally facilitators would have had formal training in the consensus process. Otherwise it is desirable that they would have had some experience as a co-facilitator with a trained facilitator.

The process starts with the facilitator stating the proposal. If some family members don't quite understand or have questions, the facilitator answers questions and restates the proposal in different terms until everyone is sure they understand what is being proposed. The proposer and others with a clear understanding of the details and intent of the proposal can give occasional help in explaining the issues.

The facilitator keeps the family on track making sure all are given a chance to voice their ideas and their concerns. Sometimes a specific topic within the proposal needs to be resolved before moving on. It is up to the facilitator to focus the attention of the family on that item so that progress is made in a timely fashion. The facilitator also refocuses people by reminding them about the proposal being considered. The facilitator declares breaks so that people can use the bathrooms, breathe and stretch. After a break the facilitator will recap what has been agreed to and what still needs work. Working with note takers, the facilitator makes sure side issues are documented for later consideration.

Note Takers

You need 'em. As with the facilitator, a good note taker should be fairly neutral on the item at hand. Otherwise co-note takers can cover for each other as each presents their ideas and concerns. Note takers query family members when they are unsure of what the person said or meant. All family members can also be taking their own notes. Audio recording can be a valuable tool for review if needed. The facilitator is never a note taker.

Mood Monitor

Mood monitoring can be done by anybody and everybody. During a discussion, people are encouraged to look at the person talking. However, a mood monitor will scan the circle watching for indications of irritability, sleepiness and restlessness. A group stretch is a good idea. You can lighten the mood with a group laugh. Breathe together loudly, hug each other, drink water, get a snack and visit the restroom. After the break, get back in the circle, ground and continue. Dancing to upbeat music for a minute or two is a good way to raise the energy level in the room and to help keep the family alert and ready to focus on what is being said.

Watch for pent up emotions. Let the family member release and process them. Unreleased emotions can be a huge block to progress. Be aware of personal attacks. You are a family and personal attacks cut deeply in a family. Negotiations where emotions run high will be tough. Deal with these issues when they come up so that progress is not halted.

One way of dealing with an issue that is a hot topic for several family members is to call a "round" to discuss the specific issue in detail. We will look at what a round is in a moment.

Timekeeper

Timekeeper is a title that is pretty self-explanatory. The timekeeper monitors the time limits – if any – on discussion topics, suggestions and proposed modifications. Ideally only the timekeeper should have a watch. However, there are people who would be uncomfortable if they are not allowed to check the time occasionally and it could make it difficult for them to be "present" for the discussion. In their case, not having a watch would be a distraction.

Peacekeeper

A family member designated as a Peacekeeper can act as a guide for new family members unfamiliar with the consensus process. They might also be called on to perform as a mediator. As with mood monitors, peacekeepers also stay alert for developing emotional problems.

Rounds

Almost everyone's hand is up. Everyone has important input to be shared about the point being discussed – right now. It's time for the facilitator to call a round. A talking stick (pillow, rock, pen, microphone or other item) is handed from person to person. Everyone else remains silent except the person holding the speaking item. If someone has nothing to say, they can simply pass the talking stick. A time limit may be set, or not, for each family member who speaks. Do not try to cover too much territory in a round. Stay focused on a specific topic. If someone goes too far off topic, a facilitator can remind them of the topic currently under discussion. There are no limits to how many rounds that may be called.

Reaching Consensus

A facilitator will test for consensus if it seems like everyone's issues have been addressed. Essentially the facilitator will ask if anyone has objections that have not been addressed. If not, the question is asked if there is consensus. It is done by asking each family member in turn. They may respond in one of three ways:

1. A family member may consent.

Consenting to a proposal means the family member will help put the proposal into action. It doesn't mean that the family member is necessarily in love with the proposal, but that they at least tolerate it because serious objections have been answered by modification of the proposal or additional information has reduced or eliminated the family member's concerns.

2. A family member may "stand aside."

This person is not quite convinced about the value or advisability of the proposal, but doesn't feel it poses a significant potential problem for the family. Standing aside means the family member will neither help nor hinder the implementation of the proposal.

A proposal can have an enthusiastic team willing to do all the work. In this case, everyone else might stand aside and the proposal will still pass. Whether the proposal is implemented depends on the continuing enthusiasm of the team. If the proposed project is not completed, that is fine. People who have stood aside have no interest in the outcome.

3. A family member may "block."

Blocking stops the consensus question cold. Use this option with care. The blocking family member and their concerns and objections are thrown into the spotlight. This may be the intent of the person blocking. Intent to block may be stated any time during the discussion to demonstrate how strong their objections are. If you state an intention to block, be prepared to talk in detail about your objections. Also be prepared to actively listen to responses to the concerns you raised. Consensus is about communication, not about wielding power.

Results

If no one blocks and everyone else consents or stands aside, the proposal is adopted. However, know that the consensus procedure is not a guarantee that all proposals will receive consensus - even if it is not blocked. The proposer might be the only one with enthusiasm for the issue. It is usually not considered consensus if everyone else stands aside. The proposer might learn things they had not considered and withdraw the proposal. When a lack of consensus seems inevitable, the facilitator can call for the process to end.

We must warn you that simply reading this quick introduction does not make you a trained facilitator or formal consensus guru. We strongly recommend that your family have at least one adult trained in the consensus process. There is a lot of information online. This review was only a brief introduction to this powerful tool.

When Consensus Goes Wrong

While visiting a cohousing group in the northern U.S., we came across a story of conflict and the continuing effort to resolve an issue. As with all of our stories, all names have been changed to protect the privacy of individuals and the community as a whole.

White Rock cohousing was created in the late 90s. The original residents had been meeting for a number of years prior to purchasing property and breaking ground on the common buildings and original housing units. Saffron had been the original driving force of the group. She advertised meetings, arranged gathering places, kept notes, studied model cohousing bylaws and researched banks and their lending practices. She effectively put her professional life on hold while pursuing her dream. In an interview, she gave us some background about her commitment to White Rock.

"I didn't know my neighbors where I used to live. I would smile and wave when I saw any of them, but I didn't know them. We never even had a block party. I missed the community I had in college. My classmates supported me in my studies. They took me out to party when I was getting too caught up in classwork. We all shared our joys, successes, failures and fears. I wanted a community again."

As with many cohousing developments, White Rock was financed using a condominium model. It made sense to the founders of White Rock because people wanted to own their living spaces and jointly own the land and common buildings. It's practically the definition of a condominium. White Rock was initially financed to build a common building and 14 small living units. The property can hold up to 19 homes. Currently 17 homes are located at White Rock.

People come and people go for various reasons. The three original community members who have left White Rock have done so for work, illness or marriage. White Rock has a fairly stable core group of 11 original members. When a home is listed publicly for sale, anyone can put in an offer. Generally when people visit White Rock to see a property, they also get a good understanding of the kind of community they would be settling in if they purchase the home.

"It is a self-selection process," says Donovan, the current president of the board of directors. "People usually get a feeling for what we are about and the kind of life we lead. We have had people who liked the area and the house but did not make an offer. One real estate agent asked us to 'tone it down.' When asked what he meant, he told us that his last prospect said not to take him to any more 'hippie, new age' communes."

"Zander, the latest person to move into White Rock, seemed comfortable with the community at first. Then his attendance at the twice-weekly communal dinners started to fall off. There were other things he did or said that made many of us feel Zander was less than thrilled with the reality of community living now that he is here.

The big break with the community came at a planning meeting. We finally have the funds in our capital improvement reserve account to install PV solar panels on the homes. Zander raised an objection about the design. Because of our northern latitude, the panels must be tilted at a steep angle to efficiently capture the winter sun. This means most homes will have racks built on their roofs to hold the panels at the best angle. Zander did not like these 'ugly structures.'

Following our bylaws, we convened a formal consensus meeting. The oversight committee presented all the facts about the solar panel project. Information about lower electric bills, fewer carbon emissions and how long it would take for the panels to pay for themselves was discussed and approved by all of the residents except Zander. He liked the idea of lower electric bills; however, he was mainly concerned about how those 'ugly racks' would affect the value of his property. For that reason he blocked the proposal."

An interesting story to be sure. We recommended that they get together with a local real estate agent and an experienced residential appraiser to ask these professionals' advice about the effect solar panels would have on the salability and value of their properties. We also suggested that they make sure that the appraiser they hire is used by the local banks. But this was just our band aid solution to a deeper problem of new people buying a condo unit and immediately having the power to block the consensus process.

To avoid having any more "Zanders" move in, White Rock might try keeping a tighter control on who moves into their cohousing development in the future. To do this they would not publicly list a vacant house for sale. Instead they would use word of mouth to let people in selected communities know of the home's availability. Perhaps a better idea is to develop a waiting list for people hoping to move into White Rock. To get on the waiting list, people would have to attend an orientation seminar. The seminars would describe the community in detail including expectations of involvement by any new residents.

Bushwick Manor, New York City

A similar private sales technique was used at Bushwick manor, a multiunit apartment development in New York City. Bushwick is a polyamorous intentional community developed in a rebuilt Brooklyn brownstone. Leon Feingold, real estate agent and developer, explains that, "all renters must be verified by an existing member of the poly community so that the house remains a judgment-free zone."

Selling through word of mouth does limit the number of potential buyers for a vacant cohousing home. It also remains to be seen if any legal challenges are brought against the Bushwick development for its non-public marketing campaign. Selling real estate (real property) is generally held to a stricter legal standard than selling your car or other personal property. Again, we feel that renting or selling by word-of-mouth is a band aid solution for a line family using the cohousing model for real property ownership. See Chapter 8, Owning Real Property for alternatives for managing real estate.

The problem we see in the story of White Rock's solar panels is the use of formal consensus for making major decisions. Formal consensus makes sense in a line family because family members hold similar values and visions for the group. For cohousing, we would suggest looking at the voting credits model or instituting a rotating planning board. With formal consensus it is easier for a person to block when they are not invested in the group's goals and vision.

Loomio Online Tool

Having an array of decision-making techniques is great. But what do you do when you have family members traveling, temporarily working in another state or your family doesn't all live on a single family compound? Look to the internet. After all, you can send emails around with issues under discussion. For a more immediate and personal touch you can make group phone calls or use Skype or FaceTime.

For a small family it works alright. Our family has used FaceTime for family meetings and it went pretty well. But then we are a family of only 4 people. We did need to plan a specific time when we would all be available. We also needed to take notes on what was discussed and the choices we made. As your family grows, finding a time when everyone can get online becomes increasingly difficult. Then there's emailing the notes everyone wrote down to some lucky family member who will collate and organize all the information and send it out to everyone. So much for the immediacy of video conferencing.

Fortunately there was an online decision-making tool being developed while we were writing this book. It currently has lots of beta testers and should be out in version 1.0 shortly before this book goes to press. The software is called Loomio and you can find it at the website, https://www.loomio.org/.

Loomio is the creation of a group of Occupy Movement activists in New Zealand. These folks saw the potential of collective decision making during the occupy protests. This potential, however, was difficult to achieve because there was no way to get everyone in the same place at the same time. Cell phones helped, but did not solve the organization problem. They lacked an on online tool that everyone with a tablet or cell phone could use.

Now that tool exists. The basic procedure is that someone sets up a group discussion where anybody can make a proposal. Proposals have time limits. People can choose one of 4 responses; agree with the proposal, disagree, abstain or block. (Note: Unlike formal consensus, blocking does not kill the proposal.) In addition to the 4 responses, you can include a short (twitter length) message about your choice. Also, as long as the proposal is open, you can reconsider the issue and change your response. Anyone can make a counter proposal as Loomio can handle several proposals at the same time. It seems to be a fairly egalitarian solution.

Lomio code is an open source software tool. Programmers from around the world are adding functionality and versatility to the program. One of the new functions being discussed is the adoption of an online brainstorming environment. Right now the software can handle groups of 300 to 400 people, more than enough for a hunter/gatherer tribe, let alone a line family. Loomio solves the problem of needing to get everyone together at the exact same time. It also solves the note taking issue in video or phone conferences. So, we suggest that you go to their website and check it out.

To Build or Not To Build:
Supporting a Non-Community Business

Philip was a founding member of the Wayward Cooperative Community. He was raised on a farm and learned construction techniques from his father and grandfather. In his twenties he earned money doing residential and light industrial construction. With this experience Philip brought valuable human capital to the construction of homes and common buildings at Wayward.

For 5 years most of Philip's time was spent on building projects for the growing community. For his efforts, he did not have to pay the monthly member dues of $425 per month. Even with that cost eliminated, Philip's savings were dwindling. One of the reasons Philip chose Wayward was because it is not far from a major metropolitan area. He likes going to movies and seeing live theatre as well as traveling. He knew he would have to start earning money because the "construction boom" at Wayward was coming to an end and he would soon have to start paying his monthly dues.

Philip decided to start a contracting business. He already had tools and a truck. All he needed was an office and a small storage facility for supplies. He visited a few real estate agents and soon found that the cost of office and storage space was more than he had planned on. So he decided to base his business on Wayward property. He could build his own office and storage space and pay a nominal rent to Wayward.

Talking privately with most of the Wayward members, Philip gave a brief description of the proposal he was going to bring to the general meeting. When the second Tuesday of the month came around, Philip went to the meeting room with his drawings and details of his proposal ready for his presentation. Things did not go as well as he thought they would.

Several members raised concerns about the proposal. Amy was concerned about nonresidents showing up on community land when they came to talk with Philip in his office. As the dress code was anything but strict at Wayward, Amy worried about rumors and gossip getting started if one of Philip's clients happened to see something that offended them. Hermes expressed concerns about toxic materials being stored on Wayward property. There were bylaws severely limiting the use of toxic chemicals on the property.

No decision was made and the issue was held over for the next meeting. The meeting's minutes were typed up and emailed to members currently living or working in other states or countries. Wayward's bylaws stipulated that to be eligible to vote on a proposal, a member must be physically present on the property. However, absent members could express their opinions by email and the email would become part of the discussion. One of the founding members, Leela, was with her mother who was sick and dying. Leela had little time or energy to pay much attention to her email and did not comment on the issue in time for the following meeting.

At the next meeting it was decided to allow Phillip to build one building that would be a combination office and storage area. The building was located as far from the common buildings as possible and as close to the property line as their zoning would allow. Parking was limited to a stall for his truck and two stalls to accommodate an assistant's vehicle and a customer's vehicle. In addition, the floor of the storage area had to be designed like a pan so that it would contain any spills the might happen. Philip agreed to everything and built the structure.

Philip pays rent and 10% of his net profits to Wayward. This outcome was not without other consequences. John had blocked. But because Wayward uses "consensus minus one" in major decisions, his single block did not stop Philip's project. John actually left Wayward a couple of months after the decision was made. John had been at Wayward for a little over a year. He felt the community was not doing enough to conserve energy and use renewable energy sources. He left to look for a community with a "greater commitment to environmental issues."

If Leela had been at Wayward during the meeting, John wouldn't have been the only one blocking the decision. Leela felt strongly that moving Philip's business onto community property did not support the community vision. She has raised concerns about people who are absent from the community not having more say in important decisions. She has proposed that a member absent for less than a year gets one-half of a vote. The no vote policy has been in the bylaws since the founding of the community. The reasoning is that someone who is not present will not have been in the private and public discussions prior to the vote and will thereby lack all the information necessary to make an informed choice.

We think that the Loomio tool might be a partial answer to this situation. It would require that people post information as it is discussed. But that is easier with Loomio than it is using email.

Comments and Conclusions

Quite a list of options to ponder. The method your family uses to make decisions and plans will no doubt vary with the size of your family, the number of businesses you develop, the number and ages of children (if any) and your relationship with other neighboring families in various community models. All of this is more grist for your family-agreements document.

We want to mention some issues around group dynamics because when you know about potential problems you can be prepared for them. In short, forewarned is forearmed. Sometimes a group will set a goal of arriving at unanimous agreement on a problem such as adopting bylaws or setting a budget. Unanimity does not equal the formal process of consensus if the rules of consensus have not been followed. Sometimes all that has happened is the dissenters in the group have been bullied or ridiculed into silence. Others might self-censor rather than be subjected to the ire of a strong, central leader. Unanimity is a high bar, which you may want to use in only the most important decisions affecting your line family.

Groupthink

In 1972 professor Irving Janis popularized the term "groupthink" in his book, *Victims of Groupthink: A psychological study of foreign-policy decisions and fiascoes*. The situation described in the previous paragraph is one example of how groupthink happens. Groupthink is the perceived or actual pressure to conform to the dominant view. The perception of pressure to conform is a difficult problem to deal with. A new line family member might be most at risk for self-censorship or thinking that they need to conform. A strong desire to belong to a group of any kind can cause a person to keep quiet and try to fit in. Trying to fit in will cause smoldering resentments to build over time. This is not a good basis for long-term relationships. Also a new member might have a fresh insight to an issue which more established members could miss. Their input could result in a better outcome than what would be created without their ideas.

In his book professor Janis lists eight common symptoms of groupthink:

"1. Illusion of invulnerability – Creates excessive optimism that encourages taking extreme risks.

2. Collective rationalization – Members discount warnings and do not reconsider their assumptions.

3. Belief in inherent morality – Members believe in the rightness of their cause and therefore ignore the ethical or moral consequences of their decisions.

4. Stereotyped views of out-groups – Negative views of "the enemy" make effective responses to conflict seem unnecessary.

5. Direct pressure on dissenters – Members are under pressure not to express arguments against any of the group's views.

6. Self-censorship – Doubts and deviations from the perceived group consensus are not expressed.

7. Illusion of unanimity – The majority view and judgments are assumed to be unanimous.

8. Self-appointed 'mindguards' – Members protect the group and the leader from information that is problematic or contradictory to the group's cohesiveness, views and/or decisions."

Groupthink will more likely happen if there is a powerful central figure that dominates the group. Severe limits on the allotted time to make a decision can cause people to jump on the 1st plausible idea presented and forego looking at alternatives. Not using an effective group decision-making technique that protects against groupthink is a path to problems.

Perhaps the most important issue facing a line family's decision-making process is that tightly knit groups are more vulnerable to groupthink. It could be due to members of the family not wanting to seem confrontational. This can lead to withholding alternative suggestions and not criticizing (constructively) the ideas of other family members.

Why is group decision making a good idea when it can be so slow and cumbersome? The short answer is involvement. When the entire family is included in developing a plan, there is more overall ownership of the solution. Everyone should understand that even if their idea was not adopted directly, it did play a part in the process. Everyone's involvement also ensures a better understanding of the issues under discussion and the resulting solution. This could be the most important reason for group decision making.

Many of the techniques we have described might seem like a lot of work. We won't argue that point with you. But do you want to make important, potentially expensive, decisions by flipping a coin? What your family gets with these techniques is the diversity of expertise and perspective of your family members. A large number of quality solutions can be produced by a line family with several members. Powerful results can be developed as ideas are evaluated and modified. We never told you that creating a line family would be easy, but rather that it would be worth doing.

Elon's Opinion on Family Decision Making

Before we started writing this book, I had no idea that so many different types of decision-making techniques existed. Mostly I had experienced the "majority rules" type of voting - one vote per person and various percentages of the vote needing to be on the positive side to carry the process forward. And then of course there is the "I don't know. what do you want to do?" method of decision making. Not a very practical way to decide something, but sometimes it happens. Every day we have to make lots of big and small decisions, by ourselves or in groups. When the group includes more than 3 people it is good to have techniques at the ready, as well as some people who have the authority to make unilateral decisions, in order to keep things rolling along. I hope that if you try some of the ideas we shared in this chapter, that it will help your family to be more harmonious and that your decision-making processes will flow easier and even be fun.

CHAPTER EIGHT

Owning Real Property

Individuals are masters of their own destiny.
So our future is in our hands.
What greater free will do we need?

Dalai Lama

Owning a house and land is not like owning anything else. It is likely the one thing you own that cannot be moved. (Yes houses can be moved, but let's not get picky.) It is also likely the biggest investment you own, unless you have held Apple™ or Microsoft™ stocks from the very beginning.

What are some of the benefits and issues surrounding real property ownership? Privacy is one issue, not just the need for an individual to have their own space where they can relax, meditate, read, do art or any of the many things which people sometimes prefer to do alone. We are talking about privacy from the outside world and all of the cameras watching us drive, walk through a shopping center and deposit money at a bank machine. Privacy from incessant advertising everywhere we look. Privacy to have a conversation without the possibility of being overheard or recorded by strangers, corporations or governments. For many people privacy is one of the largest benefits of having a home.

Owning real property also comes with responsibilities. This includes things such as keeping the lawn mowed and the house and other structures in good repair. You must make sure that food waste is secured so that it does not attract rats. This is true for both compost bins and trash disposed of by municipal waste haulers. Additions and modifications to any structures must meet minimum building codes. Building codes usually help protect the lives and property of both the homeowner and the neighbors. Richard once lived next door to a house that had an electrical fire. The wiring was extremely old and had been modified by someone who didn't know what they were doing. Sparks from the neighbor's house did fall on his roof, but luckily it had rained earlier and the fire did not spread.

Another issue is how family real estate is owned. Friends and lovers may visit and spend the night, but what happens in your house and on your land is your responsibility as a property owner. The following story is an example of how far a homeowner's liability can stretch.

A Joint Like This

Darren and Jennifer were a middle-aged couple who had been married for 18 years. Both were active in their church and Jennifer wrote and produced an annual play as a fund raising event. The actors came from the congregation. Jennifer's comedies were silly, but people enjoyed them and they made a respectable amount of money for the church. Over the years she had collected lots of clothes for costumes. It was during the start of rehearsals for her eleventh play that a potential problem came up. William, one of the actors, was unable to make the first rehearsal. He made arrangements to drop by Darren and Jennifer's house to pick up a copy of the script and his costume. William was trying on the overcoat for his costume when he put his hands in the pockets of the coat. He felt something odd in the left pocket. Standing in front of Jennifer and her husband, William pulled a joint (marijuana cigarette) out of the pocket. This was problematic as William was a police officer.

William knew that neither Darren nor Jennifer used illegal drugs. He actually laughed out loud at the looks on their faces. The overcoat had been one of Jennifer's earliest costume acquisitions. There was no way to know when the joint had been put in the pocket of the coat. William said he would dispose of the joint. He also went on to explain the "zero-tolerance" law in effect at the time. Technically they could lose their house under the zero tolerance law because that was where the joint was discovered.

As the owner you are the individual responsible for the maintenance and upkeep of your real property. You can be found liable if someone slips and falls while on your property. Guests or people subleasing a room can also create liability issues. For example, your renter has a small dog that one day decides it's a good idea to bite a small child walking by with their parents. As the property owner you might share the liability with the dog's owner.

Now let's add the complication of being the home's sole owner even though you are part of a polyamorous family of 3, 4 or more adults. A power imbalance, which can lead to conflicts over how the property is used, is created when an individual or married couple is the sole owner of a poly family home. Perhaps you believe that love and understanding will solve all conflicts that occur over the use of the property. Most likely, it won't. Suppose you own some rural property with acreage. Let's say one of your family members is a pilot and wants to build a runway and hangar for her airplane. Another member hates the idea because he wants to pasture his horses on the property and he's sure that the plane will scare them. However, you wanted to put in a small truck farm for food for the family and to sell at the local farmer's market. As the property owner you may get the final say or, if not, you may be resentful of the horses or the plane and the people who own them.

Fred's Secret

Single ownership of property might also cause a lack of community involvement. Silent Beach is one of the intentional communities we visited while we were doing research for this book. They were approaching their 20th anniversary in 2015. We heard an unusual story about this community's founding. Most of the communities we visited either had a founding group of people who pooled their money or there were only one or two couples to begin with. Silent Beach had Fred. He tells the following story.

"People kept showing up who had little or no money when we were having our initial organizing meetings in 1995. Over several meetings we had many people come and go. The ones who kept coming back impressed me. These were folks I started feeling a real connection with. All of this happened despite the apparent lack of money for any land acquisition. What they didn't know was that I had already purchased a piece of land for the new community.

When there were 10 people I felt comfortable with, I told them that the next meeting would be in a different location. We planned a carpool of three vehicles and travelled out to the property. We arrived and parked next to a cabin, which was in need of some repair. We went into the cabin where there were photos of the property on the table. Everyone was asking what was going on? I told them that this land was for sale and that for $325 per person per month they could have it. Nobody thought they could get a loan. I told them they didn't need a loan because they would be paying the money to me as I was the property owner.

Two people said no. One said they were not inspired by the property. The other person thought that I had been dishonest with them. I pointed out that it was true when I said that I didn't have a lot of cash.

Most of my money was tied up in the land. I hadn't told anyone about the property because I wanted people who felt a connection with each other and with me that was not colored by money or property.

I already had a lot of plans for the place floating around in my head. I would propose something and everyone else would go along. I would make plans for the buildings, get the permits, recruit and approve work exchange people, hire outside labor as needed and on and on. Everyone seemed to always be in agreement with my proposals. I would bring stuff before meetings and it was extremely rare that someone would question anything I suggested.

About 8 years after starting Silent Beach we were visited by someone investigating how intentional communities worked. He was a retired lawyer who wanted to learn about intentional communities so that he could set one up. He loved the tour of the property and thought it was great. Back at my house he asked who in the community dealt with the legalities, financials, special permitting, recruiting the work exchange people and other issues dealing with community operations. I had to answer that I had been doing all those functions. The lawyer looked at me and said, 'That is not sustainable.' He was absolutely right.

Since that time we have been transitioning to more egalitarian forms of community management. I think a big change in attitude happened when all the original members had paid their shares of the property cost and were fully vested in the ownership. Soon after that we put the land into an LLC. Quite frankly giving up all the responsibility of managing this place has been a relief. I have a lot more free time now." (*Note: LLCs will be discussed in detail later in this chapter.*)

It can be quite easy to let someone else do the work, especially if they have a clear vision of what they want and it matches fairly well with what the community as a whole wants. There are two ways this can become a problem. First, if the person in charge gets to like the feeling of control. It's a good idea to be leery of a person who seems to need to be in control.

Fred summed up the second potential problem well, "What if I had been hit by a bus or dropped dead of a stroke in those first few years? The community would have been thrown into disarray as they tried to figure out my filing system and hand-written notes. It could have been ugly."

We feel that Silent Beach survived having a central leading figure because his vision was one of creating a community that he could be part of. He did not find the authority that he stumbled into intoxicating as some people do. Fred was willing to work to build his dream, but he was also willing to share the work of maintaining that dream.

Where is Your Family Going to Live?

Real estate agents are taught that the three most important considerations for someone looking to buy a home are (1) location, (2) location and (3) location. In determining a good location you might want to look at the municipal codes, covenants and any home owner associations in the area where you want to buy. Municipal codes often restrict the number of unrelated adults living in a dwelling unit. New York City's Administrative Code § 27-2004 states, among other things, that there will be "Not more than three unrelated persons occupying a dwelling unit and maintaining a common household"

At the other end of our sample is Seattle, The Seattle Land Use Code sets the maximum number of unrelated people (or mixture of related and unrelated people) who may live together in one dwelling unit at eight. SMC 23.84.016. San Francisco has a limit of 5 unrelated adults in a dwelling unit. Boca Raton, Florida does not have a number we could find; however, the city has a Low-density planning directive, Sec. 28-333. The city wants owner occupied, singe family dwellings in their residential areas. We are guessing that line families would have trouble settling in Boca Raton unless they bought several adjoining properties.

Besides purchasing several residential lots, other workarounds for the maximum number of adults occupying real property exist. Your family might purchase a small apartment building. This has already been done in New York by the co-founder of Open Love NY. While the project was not created for a line family, it would work for one. The idea was to create a space where poly folks could rent apartments and live their lives free from the judgment of nosey neighbors. Other possibilities include creating a cohousing community, forming a cooperative housing corporation or just moving to a rural location where your nearest neighbor is at least two miles away.

Covenants

When considering the purchase of a particular property, make sure that you know and understand any covenants that are running with the land. Previous owners can put restrictions on how a property will be used. A previous owner's covenants will remain in effect after they have sold the property. More commonly, covenants are put in place by a homeowners association. You should know that there are two general types of covenants that run with real property. They are affirmative owner obligations and use restrictions.

An owner obligation is often used by a homeowners association to collect monthly or annual dues. An example of a use restriction is when the property is subject to architectural reviews. That means the owner must submit plans and get permission from a homeowners association before changing the landscaping, installing new siding or fences, or even painting the exterior. You also might find that your ability to rent or lease your property is restricted in some way.

Even if there is no home owners association, a disgruntled neighbor can sue you if you violate a covenant on your property. Perhaps you wanted a small tool shed or workshop installed on your property. If there is a covenant against such buildings, you can be sued by a neighbor to stop construction and return the property to its original condition.

Covenants must be legal. For example, covenants that restrict ownership of the land to people who are white, Christian or male are not enforceable. Make sure that your real estate professional has researched the zoning and any covenants so that you can make an informed buying decision.

We know of one neighborhood association that has rules restricting the unrelated adult occupancy rate of single family dwellings. Their rule is more restrictive than the local code. A large poly family ran into that issue after they bought a new home. Representatives of the family attended an association meeting as guests. After the meeting, the family decided the solution was to not join the neighborhood association. If you are not a member, their rules don't apply. However, membership in a neighborhood association is not always optional.

How Will Your Family Own Real Property?

We feel that it is important to look at group real estate ownership for two reasons. First is the situation mentioned earlier where a single person or married couple owns the property. This can create stress in the family relationship between the owners and non-owners. The second reason for group ownership of real estate is that it can keep the property out of probate proceedings when a family member dies. Group ownership does not solve the landing strip/horses/truck farm issue but it does put all the family members on an equal footing. Check out Chapter 7, Family Decision Making for methods of solving conflicts and making choices for your family.

Options exist for owning real property. Just to make sure we are all talking about the same thing, let's look at the definition of "real property." Real property is raw land and permanent improvements including structures with foundations, plants in the ground, fencing with below ground support and landscaping such as rockeries and artificial ponds buried to ground level. Affixed plumbing fixtures in the permanent structures such as sinks and toilets are also real property.

Note: Appliances such as refrigerators and stoves are not part of real property but are usually treated as part of the sale in residential transactions. Above ground pools, free standing fences and movable machinery and equipment are not considered real property.

Before we look at some options for owning real property we must tell you that we are not licensed real estate agents, bankers or lawyers. Many of the options for real estate ownership vary by state. Seek professional guidance when purchasing real estate. We are giving you our opinions about the pros and cons of various tools for owning real estate. The choice to act on our opinions is yours.

Ownership in Severalty

Ownership of real property by a single person or single legal entity is ownership in severalty. A legal entity is: single people who have reached the age of majority, married couples, LLCs, Corporations, Sole Proprietorships, General Partnerships and other organizations able to enter into contacts, sue, be sued and pay taxes. For example, you and your family do not own corporate real estate directly if the family members are shareholders of that corporation. The family controls the real estate, but it is the corporation that holds ownership in severalty. The same is true for LLCs, partnerships and trusts. We will cover this in more detail later in this chapter.

Mortgages

In French Law the term mortgage literally means "death contract." It provides for the real property to be foreclosed on if the purchaser defaults on the debt, or for the debt pledge to die when the obligation is paid off. That pretty much sums it up for U.S. mortgages too.

Banks make money by collecting interest on loans, which are usually paid in monthly installments. Monthly payments go toward reduction of the principal (the actual amount of money owed) and the interest charged by the bank or other type of lender. The monthly payment can also pay into reserve accounts used for paying real estate taxes, property insurance, mortgage insurance and any other costs associated with holding title to real property in your state. Mortgage payments do not include maintenance or utility costs. In a typical mortgage, the real property is the collateral for the loan.

We personally know of a purchase of raw land where there were 4 individuals on the mortgage, three of whom were unrelated. By default this created a tenancy in common. We will look at tenancy in common in more detail shortly. It is up to individual bank policies to set the largest number of individuals that the bank would agree to have on a mortgage. This type of multiparty mortgage has some real advantages. If one person falls on hard times, the others can pick up the slack until things improve. Lenders evaluate everyone's credit history. A less than stellar credit score will be offset by the other borrowers if their scores are good. The lender will give more weight to the primary borrower's credit score. A primary borrower is usually the person who makes the most money out of the group of borrowers.

Lenders can determine the amount that can be loaned to your group by multiplying the primary borrower's annual income by 3 and adding half of the other individual's annual income. Otherwise the lender might simply add all the annual incomes together and multiply by 2 ½. However they do it, you will get a larger potential loan amount than any single borrower would. Another advantage of multiple borrowers is the possibility of making a larger down payment. Larger down payments generally result in lower interest rates and can eliminate any mortgage insurance payment.

Mortgage Tax Deductions

One of the many benefits of owning real estate is the tax deduction for interest paid on the mortgage for a primary residence. But who gets the deduction if several people own the property? To answer that question we looked at IRS Publication 530, Tax Information for Homeowners. The information under the heading, "More than one borrower" states that for someone to be eligible for the interest deduction, they must be liable for payment and have received a Form 1098 showing the interest paid. This means that if your parents kicked in money to make payments, they don't get a deduction unless their names are on the loan.

It is likely that the lending institution will only send out one Form 1098. Let's say that there are three people liable for the loan named Carol, Ted and Alice. Carol receives the 1098 form that shows the amount of interest paid. For our example let's say Carol paid 25% of the monthly amount. If the total interest paid was $4,000 then Carol would get a $1,000 deduction. If Ted also paid 25% then he would also get a $1,000 deduction. Alice pays half of the monthly payment; therefore, she gets a $2,000 deduction.

Each person would include a copy of the 1098 with their tax return and attach a note explaining their interest in the property. The note should state how much mortgage interest they paid. The note would also include Carol's mailing address (most likely the family residence) because she received the 1098. Everyone should write "see attached 1098 and note" on the line where the amount of interest paid is written on the 1040 form. We are not sure how this would be done when filing electronically. You would need to contact your electronic filing company to see if this can be done with their product. Proportional mortgage tax deductions work on all the ownership techniques where individual "natural" persons own the real estate. Mortgage deductions are also available to cooperative housing shareholders (see this chapter's section on Cooperative Housing).

Comparison of Title Theory and Lien Theory Real Estate Sales

In a title theory state the person selling the property gives the buyer (borrower) a deed to the real estate. Next the borrower signs the mortgage and gives the title to the lender. The lender holds title to the property as security for the loan until the loan is paid in full. During the loan period the purchaser has the right to occupy the property. Once the loan is paid, the deed is transferred to the purchaser.

T = title theory / L = lien theory

In a real estate transaction in a lien theory state the person selling the property gives the buyer (borrower) a deed to the real estate. Next, the borrower signs the mortgage and paperwork authorizing a lien on the property to secure the mortgage. The buyer keeps the deed to the real estate. The lien on the property is removed when the mortgage is paid in full.

Note: Another mortgage theory is the Deed of Trust. The seller of the property gives the buyer a deed to the property. The buyer then signs a mortgage and a Deed of Trust with the lender as the beneficiary. A trustee usually holds the title to the property in trust. Title companies can offer trustee services. If your state allows, an attorney can be employed as a trustee. In this type of loan, the trustee is a neutral third party. When the loan is paid off the lender will record a Deed of Reconveyance removing the lender's interest in the property.

However, if a loan becomes delinquent, the lender can start foreclosure proceedings. The lender does this by presenting the trustee with proof that the loan is in default. The trustee then has the authority to sell the home. This type of foreclosure is fast because it does not have to go through a court proceeding.

Laws and customs are always changing. Be sure to ask your title officer about the details of a real estate transaction with a lender involved, whether buying or selling.

Co-Ownership or Tenancy in Common

Building on the previous section… If you have joined with other people who are not related by marriage to purchase real property, by default, you have a co-ownership or tenancy in common. There are some things to consider about tenancy in common:

1. Each co-owner has an undivided/fractional interest in the entire property. Normally – but not always – divided equally.

2. All co-owners can be legally forced, if need be, to pay their percentage share of the costs of owning the property. Expenses (in addition to any mortgage payments) are taxes, liens or other judgments against the

property.

3. You think your bedroom is yours? Wrong. All the co-owners have full access rights to the entire property. If one owner feels restricted from access to the property, they have the right to take it to court. If the court agrees, the other owners could be forced to pay rental for the period of the denied access to the "wronged" party.

4. Each co-owner is entitled to a share of any profits or income generated by the property. Shares are equal to the fraction of each person's interest in the property. If one of the owners sells herbs from the garden at a local farmers market, any net proceeds must be shared proportionally amongst the owners – whether or not they contributed to the effort of growing or selling the herbs.

5. No "right of survivorship" exists in this form of ownership. Each party may sell, rent or further mortgage their interest in the property. In this way a person who is not a family member could buy their way into the line family property.

6. When a partner dies, their interest in the property is part of their estate and subject to wills and probate. Again, someone outside of the family could become a co-owner. We don't know about you, but this seems like a recipe for trouble. But we're just telling you what's available. All the choices are yours. So let's look at some more options.

Joint Tenancy

What is it? Is it habit forming? Who's doing it? All fine questions. First let's take a look at what constitutes a joint tenancy. There are four conditions required for a joint tenancy to exist. No condition is any more important than any other condition; therefore, no importance is implied by the order listed here.

Same Title

All joint tenants own the property under a single title.

Equal Interest or Share

All joint tenants usually have equal interest in the property. This means equally divided equity, income and liabilities associated with the property. It doesn't matter if one person puts more money into the mortgage payment and pays for all the maintenance. All joint tenants own equal shares. Two exceptions we have found are the states of Connecticut and Vermont where proportional sharing is possible. As always, check your state laws or consult a licensed real estate broker or attorney.

Equal Rights

All joint tenants have equal access to the property and use of the property. This is the same situation we described under tenancy in common.

Equal Vestment

All joint tenants have their interest in the property for life or until the property is sold or one of the joint tenants passes away. If there were only two joint tenants, the surviving joint owner would gain full ownership of the property. The estate of the decedent would have no basis for a claim or challenge to the property title. If two or more joint tenants survive the death of a single joint tenant then the title, interest and rights are equally shared among the remaining joint tenants. Should all joint tenants die at the same time, the property is divided among the joint tenant's estates.

Note: Here are four exceptions to the joint tenancy provisions that we've heard of. For example, joint tenancy is not available to Alaskans. Alaska statute Title 34, Ch. 15, Sec 130 states, "Joint tenancy, with the exception of interests in personalty and tenancy by the entirety, is abolished. Except as provided in AS 34.15.110(b) and AS 34.77.100, persons having an undivided interest in real property are considered tenants in common."

We are told that Wisconsin has not allowed married people to own real property through joint tenancy since January 1, 1986. We have included the 1983 bill that made this change in Wisconsin law on our book's companion website www.line-family.info/CALF_companion/. Frankly we have been unable to find any text in the bill that defines real property owned by a married couple as community property with right of survivorship despite Wisconsin being a community property state. However Wisconsin Statutes, Ch. 766, sec. 31, part (2) says, "PRESUMPTION. All property of spouses is presumed to be marital property."

Oregon and Tennessee have laws that define marital property thereby eliminating the ability to own real property as a joint tenancy with right of survivorship. These four examples are illustrations of why you need to review your state laws to get the most accurate and up-to-date information.

Oregon Revised Statutes: Vol. 3, Ch. 108, Sec. 090, Item (2) reads, "When a husband or wife conveys to the other an undivided one-half of any real property and retains a like undivided half, and in such conveyance there are used words indicating an intention to create an estate in entirety, said husband and wife hold the real property described in the conveyance by the entirety."

Tennessee Code: Title 36 Domestic Relations, Ch. 3, Part 5, Sec. 505 "Tenancies by entirety unaffected."

For now let's look in some more detail about the pros and cons of sharing real property through joint tenancy. We will try to do this in the chronological order that each issue comes up.

CON: Federal Gift Taxes

When you add someone as a joint tenant, you probably become liable for a federal gift tax. We have a discussion of the gift tax in Chapter 6, Children. The gift tax applies here too because something of value is changing hands. For the sake of easy math, let's say the value of the real estate is $228,000. Note that in 2013 the gift tax exemption went up to $14,000. In a two-person transaction you will receive 50% of the real estate value, $114,000. This means you owe a gift tax on $100,000. In 2012 the gift tax ran between 18% to a max of 35% or $18,000 to $35,000 in this example. Here is one way to reduce or eliminate this tax. In 2014 every citizen had a $5,340,000 lifetime gift tax exemption. If you choose to, you can deduct the gift tax owed from this exemption amount. If your gift tax were 20% you would subtract $20,000 from the lifetime exemption. That would leave a remaining exemption of $5,320,000 in your lifetime gift exemption. Note: The lifetime gift tax exemption is often raised every year. By all means talk with your local IRS agent or tax professional.

PRO: Joint Tenancy May Positively Affect Medicaid Planning

Medicaid looks at a person's countable resources when determining eligibility. Having half-interest in a house through a joint tenancy means that only half of the home's value is counted by Medicaid. However, review how your state manages its Medicaid funds. Medi-Cal, the California Medicaid program, has a 36-month "look back period." If they suspect the joint tenancy was established in order to get benefits, they can disqualify you from assistance.

CON: Irrevocable Loss of Ownership and Control

Depending on the state you live in, one of two opposing situations occur in a joint tenancy. 1. You can do nothing with the property without the full consent and agreement from all joint tenants. 2. Any individual party to a joint tenancy can mortgage, collateralize and even sell their interest in the property. Pick your poison. The first instance might work for a line family, in that consensus should probably be the order of business when dealing with family real estate. If you live in a state where partners in a joint tenancy may not mortgage or otherwise encumber the property without the consent of all the other joint tenants, then there will be no waking up to find a stranger having breakfast in the kitchen saying (s)he wants the family to replace all the appliances.

Debts incurred against the property by a single tenant are the responsibility of all the joint tenants. This is particularly troubling in a state where an individual joint tenant can act on their own to financially encumber the real estate. For example, using their interest in the home to secure a car loan. A joint tenant's creditors or the IRS can attach the property. This is also true in the first instance, but then all of the tenants must have agreed to the debt. However, if irreconcilable differences come up, such as an individual's unpaid debts, courts can get involved and can force the sale of the property. The net proceeds of the sale – after any real estate debts are cleared – are divided between the joint tenants. That means you are going to help pay one joint tenant's bills, such as the car loan we mentioned. This leads to the next issue with joint tenancy.

CON: No Fiduciary Duty to Joint Owners

No joint tenant is obligated to act in a manner that will preserve or improve the value of the property for any other joint tenant. If a joint owner loses the property because of a debt, divorce proceeding or other issue, there is a little or no recourse for the remaining joint owners.

PRO: Relatives and Heirs Cannot Challenge a Joint Tenancy.

You could die (after a long and full life of course). In that case, your joint tenant automatically gets the house and garden. But what if you forgot to update your will that stated that the house would go to benefit the Society for Wayward Cats? Too bad for the cats; nothing in your will can break the joint tenancy. We know of no situation where anyone else has standing (a legal right) to challenge the ownership of your joint tenant.

PRO: Avoids the Time and Cost of Probate.

This is a big plus, but there are other methods that avoid probate, gift taxes and loss of stepped-up basis (a tax issue discussed below).

CON: A Surviving Joint Tenant is Exposed to Capital Gains Tax

A person's individual or community property is assigned a "step up" basis to fair market value when he or she dies. Surviving members of a joint tenancy may have to pay capital gains based on their percentage of the jointly owned property and its increased market value.

For example, let's say a joint tenant was added to a house title when the house appraised for $100,000. (The appraisal was used to determine the amount of gift tax owed.) The cost basis is $50,000 for each joint tenant. On the death of the first joint tenant, the house is sold for $200,000. The deceased joint tenant gets a step up in basis for his half, to $100,000. His estate has no gain because of the step up in cost basis. However, the surviving tenant's half has a $50,000 gain subject to capital gains tax.

CON: Simultaneous Death of Joint Tenants

If joint tenants all die in an auto accident for example (or separately within a short period of time) the property will be put through probate. There might be many heirs involved. Probate could last quite a while. In Arizona, if you die within 120 days of each other, you are considered to have died at the same time as far as your joint tenancy is concerned. Again, check with a professional who knows your state's laws.

Joint Tenancy: Now You've Gone and Done It

Let's say, for sake of discussion, that you add a person as a joint tenant to your property title. One day you were queen of your castle, sole proprietor of the income from the herb garden and unchallenged in your decorating and color schemes. Next day you add a joint tenant. Congratulations, you've just given away half of your house, garden income and linen selection authority. We really hope that this person is worth it – for the long haul.

Could something else go wrong? Yes, you could live in South Carolina… because S.C. Code Ann. § 27-7-40 requires your deed to state that the property owners hold the property, "as joint tenants with rights of survivorship, and not as tenants in common." That phrase must be spelled out instead of just using the initials "JT WROS." It's really not a bad idea to spell it out on a land deed for joint tenancy even if you don't live in South Carolina.

Are there any more potential issues to consider? Sure, if one of the joint tenants is incapacitated by injury or disease, the other joint tenant's ability to manage the property might be limited depending on the laws of the state where you live. One option you might consider is using some type of power of attorney document that comes into effect should one joint tenant become unable to manage their own affairs. However, care must be taken when granting powers of attorney. It is important to clearly spell out the responsibilities and limitations of the person named as your agent. Revoking a power of attorney can be as simple as destroying the document and notifying the person you named as your agent that you have revoked the document. Another method of revocation is to write a new power of attorney naming a new person as your agent and notifying your old agent of the change. Of course revoking a power of attorney has no effect on their ownership rights in a joint tenancy.

A joint tenant can file a petition to partition. It's a right you all have and it can force a sale of the property so that the money can be divided evenly between all the former joint tenants. Remember that all debts attached to the property will be paid before the remaining funds are evenly distributed between the joint tenants. If one of the joint tenants uses their portion of the property as collateral on a personal loan, such as for the purchase of a car or boat, it's a good idea to make sure that the loan is well documented and that all joint owners have copies of that documentation because an individual's mortgage on the joint real estate may terminate the joint tenancy. In Georgia other rules apply. See a licensed real estate professional no matter where you live.

We believe that joint tenancy is not the best choice for shared ownership of real estate. It has the advantages of avoiding probate and helping some qualify for Medicaid. However, we would look to other forms of real property ownership for a line family.

Condos, Co-ops, LLCs and Land Trusts Introduction

How should your line family own real estate? Like a lot of questions the answer is, "that depends." Each of these four methods of owning or controlling real property have their positive and negative aspects depending on what state laws are in effect and what the property is to be used for. In most cases your main concern is what your state and local laws have to say about your plans. However, there is Federal law that these four ownership methods must adhere to.

Just after the American Civil War, the US Congress enacted the 1866 Civil Rights Act. Included in the first paragraph (a single run-on sentence of 168 words) was the phrase giving all US citizens the right to, "inherit, purchase, lease, sell, hold, and convey real and personal property…" Find the full text online at, http://oll.libertyfund.org/title /2282/216253. In 1968 Congress passed a new Civil Rights Act. One of its provisions is reflected in Title 42 of the United States Code, Section 1982: Property rights of citizens. It states that, "All citizens of the United States shall have the same right, in every State and Territory, as is enjoyed by white citizens thereof to inherit, purchase, lease, sell, hold, and convey real and personal property."

However, it took the June 17, 1968 Supreme Court decision in Jones v. Mayer to fully implement the property rights of all citizens. The court decision reads in part, "We hold that 1982 bars all racial discrimination, private as well as public, in the sale or rental of property, and that the statute, thus construed, is a valid exercise of the power of Congress to enforce the Thirteenth Amendment." As we will see, these laws affect how you will manage family property and even what decision-making processes you will use.

In owning or controlling the real estate that your family will live on, it would be ideal to have exactly the right number of living spaces to accommodate your needs. But people do come and go and the living requirements for a line family will vary over the years. It is inevitable that you will end up with a vacancy or two. How you handle that vacancy depends on the financial health of your family and the immediate and long-term alternative uses for that space. First we discuss how to create a condominium project from scratch. Then we will discuss the potential for rental or sale of a vacant dwelling space when the need arises.

Condo Consciousness

One option for urban dwelling line families might be the establishment of a cohousing development. Cohousing developments are not the oddity they were in the 80s or 90s and finding lenders willing to loan on a cohousing project is not too difficult. Many intentional communities have financed their projects as a condominium. This makes sense because banks understand the condominium model and are more likely to loan money. Bankers don't want to hear about your dreams of an intentional community and would likely show you the door if you tried to explain the line family concept. So what are some of the things you should know about condominiums?

Your condo can be a group of detached single family dwellings. It is true that most condos are part of a multi-unit building with 4, 6 or more units in each structure. Old apartment buildings can, and have, been converted into a condominium, but your family is not limited to that arrangement. Of course if your "condominium" is a collection of separate structures, the amount of raw land you need increases. An urban line family will usually be restricted to a multiplex building because any residential property close to downtown will be quite expensive.

A condominium complex can be broken down into three major components:

1) the condominium unit or apartment,
2) common areas, called the general common element, and
3) limited common elements.

Individual owners of condominium units hold title to real property. As a condominium owner you also have shared access to all common areas. This could include recreational facilities, meeting halls and park-like areas. A condo owner is often assigned one or two parking spots. The owner's title usually does not include the land under the parking spot. Parking is typically a limited common element. It is generally an area assigned for your use to avoid confusion and confrontation. In some cases parking spaces are owned and can be sold, but that is the exception to the rule. Other limited common elements include things such as driveways, patios, porches and other amenities that are outside of the apartment but assigned to be used by the apartment's residents.

Condominiums are run by a board of directors elected from owners of apartments in the complex. As owners, the board members have a personal interest in the efficient and effective maintenance and regulation of the condominium property. A condominium board is not a profit making entity. In fact, the board members are usually unpaid volunteers who own apartments in the condominium. If the condominium is small enough, the board might consist of every owner of an apartment. This could work well for a line family.

Maintenance contracts for the common areas are negotiated by the board. These contracts are paid for by the monthly fees levied on each apartment owner. Because the board members are owners, they want quality work done at a reasonable price. The board also manages contracts for emergency repairs to the commons from storm damage, water main bursts, potholes, sinkholes, etc. Generally funds for these types of repairs come from a reserve account. When the reserve account is used, an extra charge can be added to the monthly condo fees until the reserve account is up to a predetermined sum. Or they might make each owner pay for their own part of the expense.

Maintaining a pleasant (if bland) appearance of the condominium is also the responsibility of the board. To this end many restrictions are placed on the outside appearance of condominium units. For example, if you own a unit in a 4-plex building, you are not generally permitted to paint the exterior of your home differently from the rest of the building. Even if all 4 units agreed to the new paint style, it would probably be against board policy. Even putting up loud colored curtains could come under the control of the bylaws.

If you like to grow vegetables and/or flowers, you may need to do that indoors because everything outside of your unit is common property and subject to condominium bylaws. If you live on the lower floor of a multi-unit structure, you may be responsible for the upkeep of a yard. Your use of the yard would likely be limited by the bylaws. The condo association will probably have something to say if you start to grow ivy and blackberries in the yard. Even some types of plants in containers on a second floor lanai might violate a bylaw regulation.

Parking can be another troublesome issue. It is common for condos to have one parking space per dwelling unit. While parking spaces are generally exclusive-use common elements, other arrangements can be stipulated in the bylaws (subject to local and state ordinances). A condo's sale price can include a parking space. In other circumstances a parking space, or two, is purchased separately. If parking spaces are owned outright by condo residents the parking spaces are not common elements. This usually makes repair and maintenance of the parking space the responsibility of the owner. A condo association might hold ownership of all the parking and rent spaces to residents. All of these situations can also apply to storage lockers.

Of course if your line family owned the entire condominium, you could make up your own rules. A common garden could be allowed. Your family might not want all the units to look the same. Your board could create bylaws allowing the individual units to be painted in various ways. To save on expenses you might set up a list of jobs for maintaining the property and require everyone to put in a certain number of hours of work on the common spaces. Your condominium could have a large common building with a kitchen. If your line family owns the condominium, it is yours to run as you see fit as long as you don't run afoul of zoning ordinances, building codes and other legal restrictions.

So how would a line family create a condominium project? We are not going to go into great detail. However we will outline an example that many cohousing groups have used in the development of raw land. Also we are assuming that there is an established line family behind this project. Please note that this is only one version of condominium development.

Step 1.

Form the legal entity that your family will use to purchase the land. This is when you should talk to a real estate attorney with experience in condominium development. To find an attorney with the appropriate background, you can take advantage of referral services provided by state bar associations and other local attorney organizations. Another option would be to ask co-housing groups in your area if they have an attorney that they would recommend. Tell your attorney that you are forming an intentional community. State your intention to finance the land as a condominium project using a legal entity.

Step 2.

Locate and buy an appropriate parcel of raw land. Take your time with this step. Not only must the property fit your technical specifications, it must be a place that your family can love. The property must be big enough to accommodate any desired family growth. If there is no access to municipal sewer lines, make sure that the ground passes a percolation test for the greatest number of people expected to occupy the property. This is needed for a permit to install a septic system. You will probably need to have some kind of conventional sewage system even if your family plans to build Earthships™ with water harvesting and reuse systems, which generate very little sewage. A lender might require a conventionally sized sewage system for the loan. Also the local building department might require it if they don't know about the water harvesting/recovery system you are planning on using. For information about Earthships, check out, http://earthship.com/. We think you will be amazed.

Step 3.

Record a "declaration of condominium" document with the town, county or parish where the land is located. Hire a real estate attorney to review, or write up the declaration to make sure it meets local and state regulations.

Step 4.

Draw up a set of bylaws. Make them conventional and in line with other condominiums in the area. This makes lending officers more comfortable with your proposed project. The bylaws can be amended later by a vote of the condominium association (board of directors) to address any specific line family issues. You can use the bylaws to spread any land payments between all of the purchasers. You could also use the bylaws to manage repayment of any construction loans by dividing the payments among the family members. Wait until after the loan is made to integrate modifications to the bylaws. These modifications can include the community garden, painting and design features for individual units, a play area for the children, etc.

Step 5.

Talk to your lending agency and tell them what your plans are. We recommend that you refer to your family as an intentional community. The banking business has a history of working with intentional communities. Also, banking institutions are notoriously conservative. Any talk of alternative lifestyles will not help your cause. If there is an outstanding mortgage on the raw land, roll it into the overall loan so that there is only one payment.

Step 6.

Create condominium purchase agreements for each of your family members. Since you are only building enough units to house current family members, the project will be sold out. Lenders like that. Banks only want to lend on projects that have an excellent chance of success. Because each family member is paying part of the loan taken out to build the project, how much should a unit cost? Depending on your local laws, you could charge each family member one dollar plus goods and services. At least one dollar is required for the sales price to family members since a contract must have an exchange of value. Because all of the family members are signed up to purchase all the proposed units, no public sale of units is required.

A note about real estate practices: In real estate there is a concept called an "arms-length transaction." That means a buyer and seller in a real estate transaction are not related by blood, marriage, business interest or any other relationship that might influence the sales price. Those are the transactions that appraisers use to determine the market value of real property. Because the line family members are integral to the project, there are no arms-length transactions between family members and the condominium legal entity. This should not be a problem. We mention it only because somebody might use the term, "arms-length transaction" and you should know what that means. As long as the money is available to pay the mortgage, most likely no one will care.

Step 7.

Publish a public offering statement. This is a declaration about the condominium that includes pertinent information about the project. This should also be looked over by the attorney as the rules are different from state to state. Each purchaser gets a copy of the public offering statement.

Step 8.

Get the loan and build your future.

———

Let's jump ahead in time a decade or two. Things will be different.

Hopefully your family has grown to its optimum size and life is good. What will you do if your family loses a family member? There are a number of reasons this will happen. But right now we want to look at the effect on the family property. Suddenly you have an empty condo unit. One strategy is to not sell or rent the property until it is needed by a new member of your family. That means everyone else in the family must pick up the slack because residences have fixed costs such as property taxes, utility hookups, maintenance and any outstanding mortgage. If your family cannot afford to pay for an empty unit, you will need to rent or sell the condo apartment.

At the beginning of this section we introduced you to the federal anti-discrimination laws when renting or selling real estate. Any local laws that restrict discrimination will also come into play. For those reasons there is little your family can do to screen who buys the condo if you have listed it with a real estate agent who uses a multiple listing service (MLS). The MLS alerts most real estate agents in your general area about the availability of your condo apartment. You can have the unit shown by appointment only. This way you can make sure that family members are always there to meet a potential resident. That way you can talk about the shared values (within limits) that the family holds. This passive screening will probably be enough to encourage people who are radically opposed to your egalitarian lifestyle to look elsewhere for lodgings. There is always the chance that they might feel it is their duty to move in and save your group from your "sinful" ways, so it is probably best to not share too much.

You could try to rent or sell the condo privately. While this limits the number of perspective renters or purchasers, it allows your family more control over who occupies the home. You must remember that even if the condo is not on the open market, it's still subject to the laws of anti-discrimination. Let your friends and acquaintances know you have a unit that needs an occupant. It is easier today to privately manage the rental or sale of a home thanks to private social networks on the internet and email lists. You can mention the potential availability of a home for rent on the online private social groups or email lists to which you belong. Advertising privately means that you are likely to get people more in tune with your lifestyle.

A real life example of private renting happened in New York City. Leon Feingold is a real estate developer, attorney and co-president of Open Love NY. (Leon sounds as if he would be a valuable person to have as a member of a line family.) What Mr. Feingold renovated was a three-story residential building with the intention of renting to polyamorous people. The initial residents of the building were found by word of mouth advertising. Lots of non-monogamous folks attend meet-ups, potlucks and other social events. By the time word got out to the media, the apartment was nearly full. That wasn't too difficult because there is a huge non-monogamous community in New York City.

Mr. Feingold has been interviewed by a number of media outlets including the Huffington Post. During that interview he was asked if renters had to be poly. His answer was very good in that it takes into consideration the federal anti-discrimination laws. When asked if someone had to be poly to rent an apartment Mr. Feingold stated that residents don't have to be polyamorous but that, "they must respect other people's boundaries." He added, "The only requirement that we have is that you not be dismissive or disrespectful of other people's life choices."

See the video interview online at: http://www.huffingtonpost .com/2014/06/16/hacienda-villa-polyamorous-housing-complex-in-new-york_n_5499723.html. You can also find the federal anti-discrimination law at, http://uscode.house.gov/view.xhtml?req=(title:42 section:1982 edition:prelim) OR (granuleid:USC-prelim-title42-section1982)&f= treesort&edition=prelim&num=0&jumpTo=true

Consider setting up your bylaws to allow for renting a property as well as selling. Renting to a potential family member would be ideal. However, renting to people who are non-monogamous themselves or are sympathetic to the concept is a good way to generate income while keeping the potential for drama low. We suggest that you don't sell a home to anyone who is not a member of your line family if you can possibly avoid it.

Cooperative Housing

Another method for owning property is creating a housing cooperative or co-op. This ownership technique was developed in New York City and is quite popular. Similar to a condominium, a co-op provides a way to manage a building, or other types of real property, with multiple dwelling units. Co-ops are governed with bylaws and managed by an elected board of officers and a director. Like a condominium, the board of a co-op sets a monthly fee to cover the costs of maintenance, repairs, insurance and utilities for the common areas. The insurance purchased by the board covers the co-op property as a whole – not the individual dwelling units. A shareholder is responsible for insuring their private living space. Next we will look at the differences between a co-op and a condominium.

First, a co-op is owned and run by a corporation. The residents do not get a deed or title to real estate. What you own are shares of the corporation. This is not common stock traded through a public exchange. Instead a housing co-op is owned by a privately held corporation that issues private shares of stock. Those shares entitle you to a proprietary lease (occupancy agreement) to one of the dwelling units.

As a member of a co-op, you pay a portion of the taxes on the property. Even though you don't "own" the apartment, you do get a federal tax deduction for the real estate taxes you pay. If there is an outstanding mortgage on the co-op as a whole, your monthly fees can also be used for paying off that loan. The portion of the fees used to pay the loan's interest could also be tax deductible. Additionally, the interest on a loan taken out to purchase your shares in the co-op might be used as a tax deduction. Consult a tax advisor. As with all laws, this can change from year to year.

A huge difference between condominiums and co-ops is that a shareholder usually cannot sell their shares or sublease to just anyone they want. The bylaws of most co-ops require that a potential shareholder or renter be approved by the board. Using such bylaws, a co-op community might be able to screen for people who share the community vision or values without violating anti-discrimination laws. This seemed odd to us until it was pointed out that there are no tenants in a co-op and there is no landlord. You don't have title to real property so that all you are selling is personal property. However, because the federal anti-discrimination law also applies to personal property, your co-op board must tread lightly to avoid problems. If a co-op board never approves a black resident, for instance, they will eventually run into a problem. However, co-op boards have been known to deny membership to celebrities because of the disruption that can be caused by media coverage and paparazzi. Is that a form of discrimination? We don't know, but we haven't heard of this being tested in court.

A typical co-op board will look at the finances of any potential shareholder. The board is looking at questions like, are they employed? Do they have good credit? Are they likely to miss monthly payments for maintenance and taxes? If someone misses their monthly payment, the rest of the shareholders must make up the difference. Because fixed costs also apply to units that are empty, the best co-ops to buy shares in are the co-ops that are nearly full.

A shareholder in a co-op is responsible for their own debts like a loan to buy their shares plus monthly fees. While monthly fees can include a payment into a mortgage on the co-op, a shareholder is not liable for a default on the mortgage held by the co-op. The co-op corporation is the responsible entity and assumes all liability should the loan go into default.

Shareholders typically have more say in the management of their property than do condominium owners. Some co-ops are set up to refund unspent money from the monthly fees that are collected. However, the IRS might look upon this as dividend profit to a shareholder and apply a tax. Check the co-op bylaws carefully and talk to a tax professional if this is an issue.

Co-op bylaws should be understood by everyone. Shareholders in a co-op may have obligations to the community spelled out in the bylaws. A shareholder may be required to get involved with the co-op's organizing committees, management or other community activities. Other bylaws can specify terms for a shareholder's maintenance of their apartment. When selling your shares in a co-op, the bylaws might state that you must sell them back to the corporation for the original purchase price. Other co-ops might let you sell for whatever rate you can get. That way you get the profit or loss on the sale. Be sure to carefully read and understand the bylaws before investing in any co-op group.

To start a cooperative housing project there first must be an investor, or group of investors that form a corporation. The corporation is the legal entity that owns the real estate. Real estate for a co-op is often a large building with multiple dwelling units. However, it could be a cluster of detached single family houses. We have even heard of trailer parks and floating home marinas going co-op. (Visions of a line family flotilla drift through our mind's eye.)

If a line family wanted to move to a new location, a co-op might be a difficult thing to sell in its entirety. We have not found any information about the wholesale transfer of a co-op to a new ownership corporation. It seems any purchaser would need to have a large number of potential shareholders lined up to move in or else the fixed costs would be divided among a small number of shareholders in the beginning. It might be possible to just open the co-op to the general public and slowly transfer the ownership shareholder by shareholder. Depending on the desirability of the real estate, the transfer could be a long process.

What happens in the event of the death of a shareholder? The following information is from the state of New York. Talk with a real estate professional for up-to-date details wherever you live. What we found is that if the shareholder was married and held the shares in tenancy by the entirety, the surviving spouse will inherit the shares.

A note to our readers in the 9 community property states: To make real estate purchased during a marriage a "community property", the property is owned as a tenancy by the entirety. This means that the surviving spouse takes full possession of their real property. If they were to divorce, the property would split evenly. Otherwise equitable division rules are applied in a divorce.

If the shares are owned by unmarried people through a joint tenancy with right of survivorship, the decedent's portion of the shares pass to the joint tenant(s). However, if the unmarried owners were tenants in common, the shares are part of the decedent's estate and will be handled in probate if necessary. Should a shareholder die intestate (without a will) the procedures in the bylaws of the co-op come into effect. A copy of the co-op's policy should be delivered to the representative of the estate. Typically the policy will detail the responsibility of the estate to pay the unit's monthly fees. When an heir is named in a will, or determined by the court, they do not automatically have the right to move into the dwelling unit. As with all other occupants they must be vetted by the co-op's board, depending on the terms of the occupancy agreement. The heir can put the shares up for sale. As with all real estate transactions, get professional licensed representation to help resolve any problems.

Is the co-op structure right for a line family? Possibly not for a rural situation. But for the urban family it is a real possibility. The property should be a good match for the size of your family. If you expect your family to grow, you might get a property that anticipates the ultimate number of partners you want. Any empty units can be leased and your family will be able to screen potential renters for a reasonable attitude about your family arrangement. You could even screen for potential new family members.

To get current information and find out more about cooperative housing, check out the National Cooperative Law Center. You can find them at: http://nationalcooperativelawcenter.com/what-is-a-housing-cooperative/the-characteristics-of-housing-cooperatives/

Limited Liability Company

In 2006 the National Conference of Commissioners on Uniform State Laws adopted a revision to the 1996 Uniform Limited Company Act. Only 11 states have enacted the proposal. In 2014, state laws regarding LLCs were anything but uniform. A state-by-state review of registration and annual fees as well as taxes can be found at: (http://thecorpsec.files. wordpress.com/2012/03/llc-annual-costs-by-state2.pdf). In looking at this list, we could not tell which 11 states were trying to be uniform with each other. This means that you should talk to a tax accountant, real estate agent or lawyer when considering purchasing family property with an LLC. Without a good understanding of the laws of your state, there could be significant unintended consequences.

Establishing and keeping an LLC can be expensive depending on the state in which you live. So why do people chose this method of real estate ownership? Privacy is one answer. Celebrities and wealthy individuals who can afford and desire privacy can use an LLC to control a personal residence. If you look up property that is owned by an LLC in California, all you will find is the name of the agent and the agent's address. You will also find the name, number and address of the LLC along with the date and jurisdiction where the LLC was filed. What you won't find is the name of the person controlling the LLC.

Along with fees and taxes, there are other monetary issues to consider. Let's say one of your family members owns real estate that is their primary residence. It is a large house with acreage where the family could live after some modifications and construction. If the owner chose to transfer the real estate into an LLC, any loans on the property could come due in full. That is because most loans include a due-on-sale or due-on-transfer clause.

Transferring a primary residence to an LLC with multiple members (other than a legal spouse) will probably cause the loss of the IRS capital gains tax exclusion. Also you will likely lose your mortgage interest tax deduction because the LLC now owns the property. In some localities the land might also be subject to a real estate transfer tax. To us this does not seem like a good way to own the line family residential property.

Most of the sources we looked at talked about using an LLC to control rental property. This is where the limited liability feature comes into play. Owning rental property has risks such as slip-and-fall claims, fire damage/injury claims, environmental hazard claims, etc. If your family controls rental real estate with an LLC, your personal assets such as vehicles, investment accounts and other personal and real property are likely not at risk from damage claims stemming from the rental property. That is because the claims are against the owner of the property, the LLC. This is how an LLC limits your liability. Often owners of multiple income properties control each one in separate LLCs providing further liability protection.

Other good reasons to control rental property through an LLC include tax advantages. Currently the IRS does not levy an income tax on an LLC. Instead, the income tax bill is passed directly to the owners of the LLC. This removes the "double taxation" that many types of corporate entities pay. If all of the owners of an LLC have equal shares, then all will claim an equal share of the income and deductions. If various owners have different percentages of the profit, each will claim that percentage to the IRS. Since membership in an LLC is by invitation and not by public offering, it seems that anti-discrimination laws might not apply. Again, talk to licensed professionals who know your state's laws to find out the whole LLC story in the state where your family controls rental property.

Land Trusts

On the face of it there is little difference between a land trust and any other trust document. The same four entities are involved:

1. the donor – who gave the land to the trust,
2. the trustee – who manages the trust account,
3. the beneficiary – who controls the property and enjoys the benefits of the property and
4. the property – aka the corpus of the trust.

In Chapter 5, Finances other types of trusts are discussed in more detail. A land trust is a revocable trust that lets individuals control real property as the beneficiary through the trustee. Other legal entities like a family controlled LLC can also be the beneficiary of a land trust.

Attachment Protection

Protection from liens against the property is one of the advantages of a land trust. Also, your position as a trust beneficiary is not in any public records. It is easier than you think to be sued by an associate in a volunteer organization for slander or liable. In a line family of 20, it is not too unlikely that someone will get in a motor vehicle accident. Even a seemingly small and uncomplicated accident can result in tens of thousands of dollars or more in claims. Without adequate insurance the property could be attached by a lien for payment of the judgment.

Perhaps your family has a custom bicycle business that builds recumbent tandem bicycles. What would happen if a customer crashed their bike and blamed it on alleged poor design or construction? Medical costs are huge, not to mention the alleged "pain and suffering" of the customer with the lousy bike handling skills. An attorney working on a contingent basis (a percentage of any awards) finding that you do not own much in the way of assets may not bother with the case or will settle for much less.

We have personal knowledge of situations similar to all those described in the previous two paragraphs. Having your real property in a land trust can protect that property from financial attacks. This is because legal matters affecting the beneficiaries of the trust should not pass through to the family property. We have seen it mentioned that one added layer of protection is to have an attorney – not a line family member – be the trustee for your properties. That way anyone attempting to find out if you are the beneficiary of any trusts would come up against attorney/client privilege. That leads directly to another benefit of land trusts.

Privacy with a Land Trust

Many people in non-monogamous relationships are not "out" in their professional lives. Some have family issues they wish to avoid. In 2015 this is the world we live in. Land trusts give you privacy because your interest in, or control of, any real estate that is in a trust will not be easily discovered. Only the name of the trust the land is held in will appear in an internet search of public records. That is because the title to the property is held by the trustee and they get title through a Deed To Trustee document. The Deed To Trustee is the only document that is in the public record and it only names the trustee and the name of the trust. The Land Trust Agreement is not a publicly recorded document. This agreement tells the trustee what their duties and responsibilities are and identifies the beneficiaries. The management, uses and profits of the property in the trust accrue to the beneficiaries.

Get thee to a real estate lawyer.

Beneficiary Inclusion

Sometimes we think that land trusts were designed with line families in mind. For example, beneficial interest can be directly given or sold to new family members. You don't have to redraw the title because it is in a trust. People's beneficiary status can be changed as needed with no public record created. As with an LLC, the beneficiary status in a land trust is an invitation only event. We don't think that there would be any anti-discrimination violations.

Building Homes on Land Trust Property

On the big island of Hawaii, land is cheap in the Puna district. There are three excellent reasons for this. First, it generally rains more than 100 inches per year. That, in combination with a lack of sandy beaches, means you will not find large holiday resorts in this area. The third reason the land is cheap is lava flows. Kilauea just passed the 32nd anniversary of its current eruption event that started January 3, 1983.

When we visited to do interviews, the town of Pahoa was being threatened by the latest lava flow that had started 5 ½ months earlier. The flow had traveled 13 ½ miles to the outskirts of the town – not a particularly rapid stream. Richard made the comment that the residents of Pahoa were strolling for their lives. As of this writing the town of Pahoa has seen little damage.

Silent Beach intentional community's land is held in a land trust. Barney, one of the founders, explains the home construction process. "Banks will not give our residents home loans because they don't own the land. The land is held in trust. If we used the trust to get a construction loan then all of the community members would be liable for the loan as trust beneficiaries. Therefore each of our residents must build their own home using their own money. But that's not the end of it. Our bylaws are written to protect the community. Part of that protection is not allowing a member to sell their house to someone outside of the community. Houses can only be sold to existing or new community members."

Wilma, another long-time resident added, "The community also limits the price that a home owner can sell their house for. I know that kept me from going too overboard when I had my house built."

Barney laughed. "Going overboard has a different meaning in our community. Wilma was considering having a covered porch all the way around her house. You have to remember that our houses are essentially bedrooms. Kitchen and general living areas are part of the communal buildings. That means individual houses don't need to be very much more than a shell to protect the occupant from rain and forest critters. Wilma had some special requirements though."

Wilma smiled and explained her situation. "I eventually settled on a porch/deck that extends around one corner of my house. It is covered. I like to be outside, even if it is raining. I don't know if anyone has told you, but it rains a lot around here. My home is a little larger than most because I also have a private art studio as part of my home."

Wilma had a building contractor build her home. She came to the community with a "fair" amount of money. Most of the community members had chosen to build their own homes because of the cost of hiring labor. Everyone must first get permission from the community about the details of their construction project. This includes the location, design, materials to be used, etc.

"Wilma is a successful commercial artist and graphic designer," added Barney. "She says that she is in semi-retirement."

"That's right. I don't look for new clients anymore. No advertising, no web page, nothing. I only work for people I have worked with before. And then only on projects that I like. The funny thing is, people now

pay me far more for a commission than when I was working full time. I
guess it's the illusion of exclusivity and living in an exotic location." She
laughed, obviously amused by the concept.

Should Wilma choose to leave the community she can sell the
house to another member. She might find that that she would lose money
on the sale because her house is too expensive for another member to buy
at its full value. The potential sales price is another factor people consider
when they build their house.

We found that most of the communities we visited on the island
either had their land in a trust or controlled by an LLC. In addition, most
of the homes and communal buildings were built by the community
members from the ground up. A few had existing buildings that were
repaired or remodeled to fit community needs. Most communities
did not consider having the trust or LLC take out a loan for home
construction for community members (partly because of the big island's
tough economy). However, a line family could use their LLC or trust to
take out a loan to improve or expand construction on family real estate.

Investment Real Estate

Maybe your line family portfolio includes investment property. We
understand that some real estate investors hold each individual property
in a separate trust account. In the unlikely event that their beneficiary
involvement in one property is discovered, all of the other properties are
still protected.

Land trusts also make loans assumable. Sole beneficiary interest
in a property can be sold – if your land is in a trust – with no public
record of the transaction. That means the lender's "due on sale" clause in
the mortgage is not triggered. The bank will notify you if the loan goes
into arrears. Make sure an attorney writes the sales document so that
the trust's beneficiary status reverts to you in the event of default on the

loan so that you can protect your credit rating and regain control of the property.

Speaking of banks and loans, there is an important item that must be taken into consideration before putting real estate into a land trust. In a land trust, the beneficiary interest is considered personal property. This means that the mortgage interest on the property cannot be claimed as a deduction on your federal income tax. For this reason we feel that a line family's primary residence should have little or no outstanding mortgages if it is held in a land trust. Income-generating real property, however, can use a mortgage interest deduction on the income tax statement of the legal entity that owns the property.

Real estate is a large financial investment no matter who you are. A line family's real property needs to be protected. We are not saying that you shouldn't pay your legitimate and reasonable debts. It's just that large sums of money are attractive to con artists and opportunists such as the auto accident "victim" we mentioned earlier. It is not unreasonable to think that an established line family, with 15 people earning an income, would represent a large amount of money. Using the average U.S. wage figure for 2010 from the Social Security Administration of $41,674/year, we could imagine an annual line family income of $625,000. However, we believe that everyone should have their own private money. So let's reduce the number by 25% and say that the annual family income is $468,800 per year. If this family has been investing in a diversified portfolio, they could have many millions of dollars in assets. A line family could be a tempting financial target for thieves.

The information in this book is not intended as legal advice. We try to provide general information only. Laws are different from state to state and change all the time. We are not experts in real estate transactions. You should talk to knowledgeable professionals such as attorneys and tax experts prior to transferring property into an LLC or a land trust. There is no such thing as a simple real estate deal. Always get competent professional help and advice before making any real estate purchase.

We gratefully welcome corrections and suggestions from licensed professionals in the areas of law, taxes and real estate. Please contact us at: director@line-family.info.

Elon's Opinions on Owning Real Property

One of the most important decisions your family will make is how the property on which your family lives is owned. That is, of course, if you live together on one property - or several properties. The land and buildings that you own will most likely be an important part of the financial holdings of the family. For that reason, they need to be protected from, well, from your family members for one thing. Especially from members that get dollar signs in their eyes when they look at property that has gained significantly in value. Not that YOUR family members would get greedy - but it does happen. I hope you will study the information we have given you, research it on your own, and then protect your family's investment in the way that seems most appropriate for your situation.

During our interviews with intentional communities, several groups told us that they felt that they were still together because the land was held in a land trust. The trusts were set up so that an individual could not sell their beneficiary interests unless the entire community agreed. This way the community controlled who gained access to the land. If individuals could have sold their interests, they might have broken up the group over the years, when things got tough. Since they couldn't sell their interest in the land, they stayed and stuck it out through the hard times - and ended up stronger for the experiences. I am not by any means saying that you "should" put your property into a land trust, but it is one powerful way to control family property. Your family – as a whole – can vote unanimously to sell your trust property. There are many reasons to sell. You might want to move to another state where the laws are friendlier for line families. Or the neighbors might be closing in, and you want to move farther out. Five-year and ten-year plans are good, but for a line family it would be good to think out a few generations. That is one of the many things that make line families different from most nuclear families - planning for longevity.

CHAPTER NINE

Homestead Skills for Urban and Suburban Families

To go out of your mind at least once a day is
tremendously important.
By going out of your mind, you come to your senses.

Alan Watts

Living Closer to the Land

What do San Francisco, Seattle and the 5 boroughs of New York City have in common? You can keep honey bees in all those locations - subject to reasonable regulations. We are going to look at some informational resources that, at first blush, might seem appropriate only for line families and others in rural settings. However, many of these skills are pertinent to urban or suburban dwellers. Who knows, you might find a business idea or two in here. At the very least you will find information that could make your line family a little less dependent on the commercial culture which pervades our lives.

Let's start by taking a look at some books and periodicals full of practical information and wisdom. The first title is "Urban Homesteading: Heirloom Skills for Sustainable Living" by Rachel Kaplan with K. Ruby Blume. You can find it at www.urban-Homesteading.org. One reviewer on Amazon.com noted that the garden section was written for a Northern California, ocean climate. However, the book also covers topics such as recycling greywater, building your own composting toilet (check your local building codes), natural paints for indoors and out, greenhouses, chicken coops and other permaculture skills for an urban or suburban line family homestead. The authors also provide an excellent list of information sources for do-it-yourself skills that can significantly lower your family's operating costs by reducing food and fuel expenses. We suggest that you check out their website.

A note about trademarks: It seems that the Dervaes Institute has trademarks on the terms "urban homestead" and "urban homesteading." This is curious since the terms have been in use since at least the early 70's in The Mother Earth News magazine. We initially called this chapter Urban Homesteading, but we will honor the peculiar ruling that awarded these trademarks to the Dervaes Institute because we do not want to get involved in any legal action. Therefore we will not use those terms. (That doesn't mean that we accept the validity of trademarking such a commonly used expression however.) The Dervaes Institute owns a number of websites who's URLs begins with "urbanhomestead.org/..."

Before buying any books, check out the information that you have already paid for (if you live in the U.S.). It is online at, http://afsic. nal.usda.gov/farms-and-community/urban-agriculture. This site has over a dozen links to pdf books such as "Urban Agriculture – Best Practices and Possibilities" and the "Urban Farm Business Plan Handbook." Other links take you to resources that will help your family learn about urban agriculture. For example, the site has a link to the USDA People's Garden blog, and to the USDA Urban Soils Issues website, as well as lists of references and resources.

We are also interested in Thomas J. Elpel's work on simple living and simple and elegant home building. He uses low-cost methods and materials to build passive solar homes. Passive solar heat does not use motors, pumps or ductwork. This eliminates a lot of the extra costs found in active solar heating systems that rely on technology to operate pumps and valves.

Elpel points out that building your own homes and communal buildings will save interest payments on a mortgage. That is worth 10s or 100s of thousands of dollars. As Diana Christian says in her book "Creating A Life Together", your family members' work is the same as money. What Tom Elpel adds is that it's tax-free money. His work is at Hollowtop.com. He has published a number of books. We are planning on getting one or two of them to read and do a proper review. Stay tuned to www.line-family.info/CALF_companion/ for this and other reviews.

Magazines have been tracking the progress in energy efficiency, local food production and renewable energy for decades. If your line family is "Gonna Move to the Country, with a half a dozen lovers" then you can't do much better than a subscription to the Mother Earth News. All of the back issues are available on disc and new issue subscriptions have the option of digital only delivery. Richard owns the first 75 printed issues. The first issue was published in January of 1970. You can find out about this remarkable resource at Motherearthnews.com/.

Since July of 1985 "Permaculture Activist" magazine has been documenting the permaculture movement. It gives up to date information on techniques and tools. The site's introduction describes their mission very well, "We supply information that enables people everywhere to provide for their own & their communities' needs for food, energy, shelter, & to design decent lives without exploitation or pollution & from the smallest practical area of land." Get more information at, www.permacultureactivist.net/.

If you have read "Sex at Dawn" by Christopher Ryan and Cacilda Jethá, you know about the destructive changes in civilization and the environment brought on by the advent of agriculture 8- to 12-thousand years ago. There are agricultural technologies however, that work with nature to produce crops that are organic and plentiful. "Masanobu Fukuoka's Natural Farming and Permaculture" by Larry Korn will give you some ideas about what is possible when people work with nature rather than trying to conquer and dominate the world. Fukuoka's results are amazing. Mr. Korn's article can be found at the following website, http://www.permaculture.com/node/140. Masanobu Fukuoda's book, "The One Straw Revolution: An Introduction to Natural Farming" can be purchased at Amazon.com.

A Web of Information

Websites can provide excellent information too. Here is a website full of information and resources, which you and your suburban or urban dwelling line family may find useful, http://iuhoakland.com/. This website lists many hands-on classes in the Oakland California area. If you are in the neighborhood of Berkley or Oakland, you might want to take advantage of their expertise. If you don't live near, or travel to, Oakland very often there are many other websites devoted to classes on urban farming and other self-reliance skills in most major urban centers. Here are just a few more –

Denver CO. http://www.denverurbanhomesteading.com/

Portland OR. http://portlandurbanfarmproject.wordpress.com/

Detroit MI.   http://detroitagriculture.net/urban-garden-programs/
              adult-education-programs/

Charlotte NC. http://www.sowmuchgood.org/urban-farm/

New York NY. http://www.justfood.org/farmschoolnyc

For a more general and overall look at city farming, self-sufficient living and conservation, check out the following sites:

http://www.cityfarmer.info/

http://greenliving.lovetoknow.com/Self_Sufficient_Living_Tips

http://www.selfsufficientish.com/main/

If you only have a patio or balcony you might look into vertical gardening techniques. Even if you only have a few square feet of yard space available, a vertical garden can add significant production to your limited garden area. Check out some interesting ideas on the website, http://theselfsufficientliving.com/vertical-gardening-ideas-designs-and-plans/.

We love the Urban farming guys. They have some great do-it-yourself videos that are not only informative, but entertaining as well. Topics include aquaponics, composting, worm farming, food preservation, solar power, methane bio digesters and much more. Find this site at http://theurbanfarmingguys.com/.

Dorothy Ainsworth is a prime example of living life well while having a minimal environmental impact. You can read her story at http://www.dorothyainsworth.com. She is a firm believer in the art of scrounging. Her website gives lots of tips for finding inexpensive or free building materials. While she lives in a rural setting, her techniques for finding low-cost materials, home furnishings and tools are also useful for urban and suburban families. It's an inspiring story of living life on your own terms.

About.com is a fascinating and extensive website. This site has 1,000s of subjects, which are easy to browse. Prepare to spend a lot of time on this site. Following are a few subjects that we specifically chose to help people become more independent of the consumer culture and take responsibility for their ecological impact.

Soap Making

Sewing

Food Preservation

Fishing

Gardening

Candle Making

Note: Candles can be made from various materials. Two common types of candle wax are paraffin and beeswax. Paraffin is a petroleum based product, a fossil fuel. In a reasonably tight home this can cause indoor air quality problems. We prefer beeswax, a natural and renewable form of energy. Vegetable palm wax is another renewable candle alternative. Still any open flame inside a house can put unburned hydrocarbons and particulates into the air that might cause problems for people with respiratory issues. Also there is the danger of fire.

"PermaculturePrinciples.com" is a good resource for learning about the full range of permaculture topics. Permaculture is often old knowledge being used for a new culture. This new culture recognizes old truths. For example, mankind is not apart from the world, but a part of the world. Instead of conquering and taking, we must learn to share and give back to nature. You can find lots of information at the Permaculture Principles website.

A word of caution: free information abounds on internet websites; some of it is accurate and well presented; some of it is incomplete, misleading and confusing. We have tried to stay with the established information sources that have proven reliable. Still, even the most trustworthy sites can have erroneous information. Before spending lots of money and time on a large project, double check the information with independent sources.

A Fair Place to Learn

You can find lots of good advice and information in the real world too. Don't forget your annual county, regional and state fairs. They are generally held in the late summer or early fall. You will find lots of information about your region from individuals and groups presenting at a fair. They have experience with what works for gardening in your climate and soil conditions. You can probably find out about regulations regarding animals that you can keep in your city or suburban location.

There will likely be conservation and solar energy businesses at the fair. Many times these businesses have free classes and literature about how to use conservation and renewable energy. Seeing what other urban and suburban residents are doing will give you ideas and support for your family's efforts to become more self-sufficient.

The websites, books and periodicals we have mentioned all have knowledge and inspiration to spare. The inspiration part can lead some people (Richard) into jumping into the deep end and taking on more projects than can be reasonably handled in the time available. It's not that we are saying you should only do one project of the many available to urban residents, but understand that each project takes more time to set up and get started than it will to maintain after it is running. It's just a friendly note to the overly ambitious folks to not become overwhelmed and discouraged by taking on too much too fast.

Elon's Opinion on Homestead Skills for Urban and Suburban Families

For me, one of the most exciting things about line families is the variety of people who will be involved. Each person will bring their own set of skills and interests. Richard and I tend to be the type of people who are interested in a lot of things - more things than there is time in life to pursue. Some of those things I'm perfectly happy to watch from a slight distance. Other things I want to get right in there and experience myself. Eating organic vegetables from the garden without having to actually work in the garden myself (not pleasant with a bad back) sounds great to me - especially if the people tending the garden love doing that.

One of the big advantages of living in a line family is the economy of scale. Also it is much less expensive when the family has members who can do creative projects and repair work for the family. And all of the food that you grow or raise saves you money as well as giving you more control over quality. In the process of exploring urban permaculture and self-sufficient living, your family may find another income stream through a family business.

CHAPTER TEN

Random Notes

The cave you fear to enter
holds the treasure that you seek.

Joseph Campbell

Most people we know have a junk drawer. It's often in the kitchen, but can be in a den, living room or any other room within the main living area. A junk drawer is where you find the odd tools, note pads, office supplies, etc., which don't seem to have a better place to live. The term "junk drawer" is a misnomer since anything you need is not junk.

Random Notes is our junk drawer. Topics and ideas that did not fit comfortably into a chapter, or that are tangential to the main topic, are found here. We think you will find some interesting ideas, amusing thoughts and useful tools.

On the Word "Polyamory"

We use the term polyamory often in this book. We also use the terms non-monogamous, ethical non-monogamy and non-exclusive relationship. We realize that there are some non-monogamous people who don't use or like the word polyamory. Some feel that it has been co-opted by the media to mean young, usually attractive people all living under one roof. Others have seen posts on social media that argue about the 'right way' to do polyamory and don't want to be involved in those disputes and neither do we. But just to be clear, our definition of polyamory includes concepts such as choice, honesty, consent, communication, self-determination and egalitarianism. Please forgive our use of the word if you are uncomfortable with it. It is how we refer to ourselves and it is quicker and easier to say and type on a keyboard. And we're not that offended by mixing Latin and Greek roots.

On Magick

(Not to be confused with the magic performed by entertainers such as Penn & Teller)

In Chapter 7, Family Decision Making there is some magick included in the description of the process of Formal Consensus. We mention creating a safe space, forming a protective circle and breathing in unison. This may seem like superstitious nonsense to some people. We beg your indulgence for just a few moments as we describe some real magick that was proven by science to work. Many people for years have believed that planting seeds by the light of the full moon produces a better crop yield. Where does this belief come from?

Agriculture started roughly 10,000 years ago. This was long before electric lighting, mechanized farming, insecticides and herbicides. Picture these ancient farmers planting their fields. It took a lot of labor and time. For a large farm it could take more time than there was daylight to get the seeds planted. But if you have a moon that is nearly full and a sky without clouds, you have enough light to turn dirt, place seeds and replace the dirt. It's a pretty simple operation.

After several years, or generations, the farmers started to notice that the fields planted by moonlight produced more than the fields planted in the daylight hours. The conclusion was that planting at night by moonlight is a good idea. Human beings can't just leave unexplained things alone. We like to have reasons for things happening the way they do. We make up meanings when the reasons for events are not evident.

Several thousand years ago they did not have microscopes, laboratories or scientists who would know what to do with microscopes and laboratories. So they made stuff up. Gods caused the thunder and lightning and the moon had power to help things grow. No matter the meaning applied by humans, planting by the light of the moon worked and fields planted that way produced more.

Science came along and started learning all manner of stuff. Science has become somewhat arrogant and usually dismisses many of the old ways out of hand, calling them primitive or old wives' tales. However, a study done by the Agricultural Research Service in Iowa found a link between weed seed germination and exposure to sunlight. They determined that tilling the soil (which brings weed seeds momentarily to the surface) was best done at night by a new moon (when there was as little light as possible). Tilling in the dark led to less weed seed germination and thus to fewer weeds in the field competing for water and nutrients. Planting by the light of the moon results in fewer weeds allowing a higher crop yield.

So maybe a group breathing together in unison or casting a circle seems primitive and unscientific, but it seems to work for many people. And what's the harm in deep breathing or casting a circle? It doesn't have to "mean" anything. If it works for you, it works. If it doesn't work for others, it doesn't work. Just remember the story about planting by moonlight before you dismiss people who include "magick" in meetings and rituals as lunatics. They just might be onto something.

On Legal Recognition for
Non-Monogamous Relationships

We think that the first step towards any type of legal recognition of consensual non-monogamous relationships is a national single payer healthcare system. It eliminates one of the major financial arguments against polyamory, namely the cost to businesses of insuring an employee's multiple spouses. Of course corporations don't currently limit the number of children that are covered in an employee's medical plan. But logic is not always the basis of corporate policies.

Must All Line Family Members Live Under One Roof
(or next door to each other)?

We respond with a resounding NO. Our family of four has only lived under one roof when on family vacations. It seems that a non-monogamous family all living in the same building is the "gold standard" for some people. We are here to tell you that there are happy poly families that live in houses separated by a mile as well as families that are sometimes separated by a continent or an ocean. This is your life. You and your family get to make the rules. If your dream is to all live in a large apartment building or in a sprawling ranch home, go for it. Just know that it is not a requirement. Richard's "gold standard" for a poly family or line family would be adjoining – not connected – housing. There would be central facilities such as a media room to watch movies on the family theatre system and a communal kitchen with all the great kitchen gadgets. Sound like a cohousing model? It is.

Elon on the other hand wants us all to live near a beach on Maui, where is it just too warm for Richard's taste. If we ever decide to all live on Maui, one possibility for us would be for Jim and Elon to live near the beach and for Richard to live "upcountry" where it is cooler. Judy might choose one or the other, or move between the two. Your family might also need to consider similar needs of its individual members.

The amount of personal space each person will need is a consideration. As we are writing this book, Richard is living in a 200 square foot space. He was used to much greater personal space earlier in his life, but circumstances and needs change. Half of the year he shares those 200 square feet with Elon – a true test and sign of their commitment to, and love for, each other. You might not want to try this at home.

Can People Who Are Not Poly be Part of a Line Family?

Our guess would be no and yes. The "No" comes from our definitions of intimacy in Chapter 1, Intimacy. If the new member reserves their sexual intimacy to only one person, we would expect other forms of intimacy to be shared with the other members of the line family. If other types of intimate interactions with the family were not established, we would have strong reservations about admitting this person into the line family. We base the "yes" on the fact that we know some successful mono/poly relationships. It falls under the concept of everyone being at choice about their own types and levels of intimacy.

To take it one step further, we believe that a celibate person could do quite well in a line family. We know of a female triad where one of the partners is asexual. This does not mean that she is not a passionate and loving person. Quite the opposite, she loves cuddling with her partners, snuggling and hugging them often. Being asexual does not mean that you don't like or need the touch of other people. We think that the perspective of an asexual person would actually be quite valuable for a line family.

Further Evidence of Family Power and Influence

1. One of the most powerful political groups on Earth was detailed by Jeff Sharlet in his book "The Family: The Secret Fundamentalism at the Heart of American Power." Young men and women are groomed for addition to The Family if they show the proper attitudes being sought. The Family also networks with established politicians and military commanders all over the world. The Family has gained enormous, world-wide political influence and wealth.

2. In 1789 the U.S. Congress started holding regular sessions. House and Senate historians recently compiled data that revealed an interesting fact. In its history (as of 2014) Congress has, so far, seated around 200 members who have subsequently had a child, or children, elected to the House or Senate. In addition 190 pairs of siblings have served in Congress. All this despite the Constitution's attempt to ban the inheritance of power through bloodlines such as through the conveyance of a title of nobility; "*No Title of Nobility shall be granted by the United States: And no Person holding any Office of Profit or Trust under them, shall, without the Consent of the Congress, accept of any present, Emolument, Office, or Title, of any kind whatever, from any King, Prince or foreign State.*" U.S. Constitution: Article 1, Section 9, Clause 8.

3. Author Stephen Hess looks at some of the longer lived families in his book, "America's Political Dynasties". Hess profiles sixteen influential political families from colonial days to the end of the twentieth century. The author demonstrates that political inheritance is a fact in US politics and sheds light on the stories of 200 politicians who have benefitted from a recognized family name in their bids for public office.

Planning for the Unexpected – Babies:

Short of abstinence, sterilization is the most effective method of birth control. However, occasionally even people who have gone through a sterilization procedure get surprised. Oh, and just to be clear, we do not recommend abstinence. It is probably unhealthy. Even so, it is a matter of personal choice and we believe that it should be respected. Unexpected pregnancies are one of the many reasons your line family should have a healthy emergency reserve fund. Raising a child not only takes a village, it takes a lot of money as well.

Planning for the Unexpected – Economic Collapse:

Your family will probably have people with marketable skills. You'll be ok. Don't go outside for a week or two. Don't be in debt. It is always good to have some food and water stored. But don't go all survivalist on us.

Planning for the unexpected – Zombie Apocalypse:

Shotguns! Nothing puts a zombie down like a 12 gauge. However our partner Judy prefers her samurai style katana sword. She says, "It never needs to be reloaded." Can't argue with that.

Planning for the unexpected – Power Failure:

There is nothing like a generator to make you feel smug until the gasoline runs out. Have a high quality refrigerator and freezer with good insulation, then open and close them quickly when you need to take something out. Use all the fresh and frozen food first before opening the dried and canned foods. Better still, have some renewable sources of energy such as a wind turbine, photovoltaic solar and solar domestic hot water. If you are in an area with regular power failures, you might also want to install some electrical storage batteries.

Make sure that your lighting systems and appliances use energy efficiently. Currently LED lighting is the best for efficient general illumination. We use LED lights in our homes and like them a lot. Also, spending a little more money on good quality efficient appliances will save money in the long run.

Planning for the unexpected – Pandemic:

Surgical masks and gloves, your own personal towel, a good medical plan; these are a few of our favorite things. Don't forget the hand sanitizer.

It Usually Seems Like the Unexpected Things You Must Plan for Are Always Horrible

A sudden outbreak of world peace hardly needs to be prepared for. How about all diseases suddenly being cured? Hey - prepare for a party of epic proportions.

On the Transfer of Real Property Between Individuals

Transfer of real property by a will can be challenged. If you plan to put your home in a revocable trust, you are well advised to have a lawyer draw up the paperwork. That will cost you money. The cheapest and most secure way we have discovered to make sure your home goes to the person(s) you intend is to use a Transfer on Death Deed. Check to see if this option is available in your state.

Washington State Transfer on Death Law is found in:

Title 21 of the RCW, Chapter 21.35 Uniform transfer on death security registration act, 005 – 902

See Chapter 8, Owning Real Property for a discussion of group ownership and transfer of real estate.

Legalese: Why do Lawyers Talk Funny?

What is meant by the term "legalese?" One police officer we know told us that, "Lawyers are just people you pay lots of money to go into court and speak Latin." Up to a point, that is true. But why is so much Latin used in the law? You might also have noticed that Latin is used in science and medicine. The useful thing about Latin is that it is a dead language. That means the definitions of words are set and don't change. You don't find slang terms in Latin. Except for a few terms such as 'carpe diem' for seize the day or 'caveat emptor' for buyer beware, you don't find many people knowingly speaking Latin in everyday conversations. The result of using Latin is that Judges and lawyers know exactly what each other are saying in a courtroom. It makes for clear and concise communications; and we know how valuable that is.

On Robert's Rules of Order

We don't discuss Robert's Rules of Order in Chapter 7, Family Decision Making for two reasons. First, there is lots of free information available about the process on the Internet and in public libraries. Second – and most important – Robert's is designed for adversarial politics. It is a system that usually keeps politicians with profound differences of opinion from shouting one another down or worse. Even with those rules in place, things can get out of hand. For example, on May 22, 1856, Senator Charles Sumner was beaten with a cane by Senator Preston Smith Brooks on the floor of the U.S. Senate. Sumner was severely injured taking 3 years to recover enough to return to his duties as a senator. Hopefully your family will not have such dramatically divergent views on important subjects that you will need the protections of Robert's Rules of Order.

On Communes

In the 60s and early 70s, many young people who were fed up with the Vietnam War, pollution, lack of civil rights and politics in general dropped out of society and formed communes. This was labelled as a "back-to-the-land" movement. Most of the communes formed in the 60s failed. City kids didn't know much about gardening, let alone farming. They didn't know how to can or otherwise preserve food and they found out that living in a close-knit community of strangers wasn't all that easy.

But some communes succeeded. Some of the intentional communities around today started as communes. Some intentional communities bear a striking resemblance to 60s communes. The word commune has fallen out of favor. It is a word with a lot of social baggage. In reality, communes have existed in the U.S. since its beginning and will likely exist far into the future. Some people just have to make their own rules.

On Taming the Wild Community Meeting

In its beginning the Lahar Creek Creative Community had daily meetings. These meetings would typically last at least 2 hours and occasionally stretched to 4 hours. Everyone was skilled in the use of nonviolent communication (NVC). What they weren't skilled in was planning and running a meeting. Lisa gave us some of the details.

"A lack of focus is what I most remember about those meetings. We would talk about chores and projects that needed to be accomplished.

Some people would jump in and talk about the things that they had accomplished related to their personal goals and desires. Stories about events unrelated to the community would be told and some would start a heart share. The meetings were horribly inefficient. To make matters worse, every decision was run through the consensus process. Even small matters like deciding if we should only use white balls for our Ping-Pong table could take 20 or 30 minutes to resolve.

Eventually we found that fewer meetings were needed as matters in the bylaws and general maintenance and operation of the community were resolved. We started having one business meeting a week. Instead of making all decisions through consensus we make less critical decisions by voting. The votes usually require a substantial majority of 60 to 75%. To keep that meeting focused on business, we scheduled a weekly story sharing time when people can talk about their experiences as a community member. In addition, we have a Monday morning check-in for people to talk about any goals, concerns or issues they think need to be addressed in the upcoming week. This is normally when people work out swaps with other community members on their chore schedule or ask for assistance on personal projects like maintaining their homes."

We think that as a line family grows, the issues around the types and lengths of formal meetings would evolve naturally to fit the needs of the family. In this story we see the importance of the ability to adapt to changing needs and desires. Traditions are nice as long as they serve a purpose or are entertaining. A lack of flexibility can tear a community apart. It is probably the same for a line family.

On Dietary Issues

We were told, at a surprising number of communities, that basing a community on a dietary regime is a sure recipe for failure. Apparently just because everyone is an ovo-lacto, gluten free, pescetarian it doesn't mean that you will all get along. It also does not mean that you will all continue to follow a particular dietary plan.

While visiting the Moonstone Meadow intentional community we heard about a dietary issue that didn't work out. Moonstone's kitchen is well equipped and can easily segregate vegan and vegetarian food from meat products. They just weren't prepared for Peggy, a work exchange visitor in 2014. Luanne, the 'kitchen goddess' explains what happened.

"None of our members had any experience with raw food diets. So when we received Peggy's work exchange application form, we didn't think twice about the raw food diet she said that she followed. We learned soon enough about the disruption a raw food diet would cause.

Now you must understand that Peggy was a delightful person. She had lots of enthusiasm and put in a good solid day of work. I calculated her daily Calorie requirement at around 4,200. What I didn't realize at first is that raw foods are harder to digest. That means anywhere from 10 to 15 percent of the food's Calories are used by the body in digestion. So she actually needed almost 5,000 Calories of food per day."

Luanne had picked up her kitchen information notebook. "A half a pineapple has about 110 Calories, an orange around 60 and a mango about 147. A large avocado will give you around 360 Calories. A cup of almonds is 820. A cup of walnuts is 780. A cup of sunflower seeds is 810. The shear bulk and expense of her diet did not work for us. Luckily we found her a work-exchange position at a community where they mostly eat a raw food diet. She was here for a week. Man did we have extra scraps for the compost pile."

Not Lovers… Whatever

Richard here, and I just finished watching a television show about polyamory from Australia. The program focused on the relationship between a man and two women. The narrator went into some detail about terms used in poly saying, for example, that the three people involved were not a true triad because the two women were not intimate (having sex) with each other. Otherwise they get along fine with many common interests. One of the women said to the other, "Love you to pieces, but we're not lovers." The other woman nodded her agreement.

My brain is tying itself in knots trying to parse this statement. I know that the term "lovers" generally refers to people who are sexually intimate. But with that generalization we are limiting what love is and can be. It was just odd to see two people who obviously felt love for each other and sharing some type of intimacy saying that they were not intimate.

Sexual intimacy is important, but does it trump all other intimacies? Our society devalues other intimate ways of relating through emotional connections, intellectual or creative collaboration, mutual spiritual experience or the closeness of non-sexual touch. I was saved from severe injury and possible death by the unflinching trust I had for a person with whom I shared a recreational intimacy.

The three people in relationship may call themselves a triad, truple, V, triangle or anything else they want to call themselves as far as I'm concerned. However, these terms seem to be defined by sexual connections. The sexual dynamic of a relationship can change over time. I can see the Facebook post now. "Just wanted to let everyone know that we are no longer a truple, we are a triad." I would rather that they would just clearly state that they are all sexual with each other now. But then, perhaps it isn't the business of the whole world to know what the configuration of your sexual relationships or any other intimacies are.

If you have any ideas that you think should be added to the Random Notes chapter, send them to director@line-family.info. We just might add them to the website.

Elon's Opinion on Being Poly...
in a World that Thinks It Is Monogamous

As a poly person, never apologize for who you are and how you live your life. I have had very few problems with people being upset when they hear about my lifestyle - almost none, outside of relatives. I think the reason that people do not react negatively is because I state it as matter-of-factly as I talk about where I work, my hair color, my height, etc. It is simply part of how I express myself in the world. I don't give them any reason to think that I should be judged for my behavior, so they don't (at least not to my face). In fact, most people find it interesting and ask me questions. Some of the questions might be considered to be rude, if I was so inclined to see them that way, but I usually don't. I am comfortable with my decisions and that allows others to be more comfortable, and even to often share something about themselves that they might otherwise feel nervous about sharing. If you are in a work situation where it is just not safe to share information about your lifestyle, that is unfortunate. I'd suggest that you share, where you can and with whomever you can, to find your community of like-minded people. It helps!

CHAPTER ELEVEN

Cohabitation Arrangements

The law isn't justice. It's a very imperfect mechanism.
If you press exactly the right buttons and are also lucky,
justice may show up in the answer. A mechanism is all
the law was ever intended to be.

Raymond Chandler (1888 -1959)

You have to be lost
to find a place that can't be found.

Captain Barbossa

Back in the '80s Richard was appointed co-executor of his father's estate, with one of his sisters. He had to talk to a lawyer several times because his father used a will to manage most of his affairs. Richard's longtime partner Wendy (not her real name) was with him during his last meeting with the lawyer for the estate. The lawyer knew that Richard was legally single. When he found out how many years Wendy and Richard had been cohabitating, he warned them that their finances were legally entangled. He said that either one of them could file claims against the other should they ever break up.

Richard didn't understand how there was a legal connection between Wendy and himself since Washington State never had a common-law marriage statute. The attorney insisted that there were potential problems for them. They didn't pay any attention to his warnings. Richard and Wendy did eventually part. It was painful but neither of them sued the other. However, the lawyer was right; they could have taken each other to court over the distribution of co-owned property.

Meretricious Relationship

What the lawyer had failed to mention was Washington State's concept of meretricious relationships. The term "meretricious" has historically been used in many states to label and define the cohabitation of unmarried adult couples. This term has a negative connotation; meretricious is actually an adjectival form derived from the Latin noun meretrix, which means registered prostitute. Now the Washington State courts call a couple's cohabitation a "committed intimate relationship."

Unlike common-law marriage, couples in a meretricious relationship generally have few of the benefits of marriage such as filing joint tax returns or patient visitation rights. Instead couples in a meretricious relationship have the right to file lawsuits against each other if the relationship ends. The potential legal problems are occurring more frequently as more and more people opt for cohabitation either prior to marriage or as a substitute to marriage. In addition, states are backing away from recognizing common-law marriage and adopting the concept of meretricious relationships. In most states this leaves unmarried, cohabitating couples with none of the legal benefits of marriage, but many of the hassles of divorce.

Common-Law Marriage

As of this writing there are only 10 states and the District of Columbia where you can form a common-law marriage. The 10 states are Alabama, Colorado, Iowa, Kansas, Montana, New Mexico, Rhode Island, South Carolina, Texas and Utah. In New Hampshire common-law marriage is only recognized for spousal estate inheritance through probate. The following states only recognize common-law marriages created before a certain date:

> Ohio if created before 10/10/1991,
> Idaho if created before 1/1/1996,
> Georgia if created before 1/1/1997 and
> Pennsylvania if created before 1/1/2005.

Oklahoma's statutory law seems to be in conflict with some state court rulings. We have been unable to find any definitive information as to whether common-law marriages formed after 11/1/1998 are valid. Couples in Oklahoma need to keep an eye on this issue.

A typical common-law marriage myth: After seven years of cohabitation you are married. No state in the U.S. has ever had a "seven-year" rule. We are not sure where this idea came from (and out of curiosity we've spent a little time looking). In the dwindling number of states that recognize common-law marriage there are various tests to tell if you are simply roommates sharing rent, or in a marriage-like relationship. For example, have you and your partner cohabitated continually for longer than two or three years? Do the two of you hold yourselves out to the public as married? Have you and your partner comingled your finances by filing joint tax returns or establishing a joint checking or savings account? Answering yes to any of these questions can be used as evidence of a marriage-like relationship.

In addition to the conditions outlined above some states want proof that the couple has had sexual relations and that they have been "exclusive." We wonder (and are worried) about how a state might collect evidence of a monogamous sexual relationship.

A few states do grant some state-level spousal rights to cohabitating adult couples. Those states are California, Oregon, Nevada and Washington. The District of Columbia as well as Hawaii, Maine and Wisconsin provide almost all state-level spousal rights to couples with cohabitation agreements. Please note that these lists of states and the rights provided are subject to frequent change. For more current information, go to our website at: http://www.line-family.info/CALF_companion/. With your help we will do our best to keep it up to date.

Another thing you should know is that in 20 states (as of January 2, 2015) adultery is illegal if one or both of the parties are legally married to another person. The states are Alabama, Arizona, Florida, Georgia, Idaho, Illinois, Kansas, Maryland, Massachusetts, Michigan, Minnesota, Mississippi, New York, North Carolina, Oklahoma, Rhode Island, South Carolina, Utah, Virginia and Wisconsin. New Hampshire's adultery law was struck from the books on January 1, 2015.

All of this means that if you are an adult living with another adult in a romantic relationship, you're possibly an adulterer or in a legal meretricious relationship – both defined by the state. What to do? Take charge of your personal life. In states where adultery is illegal, there are two things you can do to change your situation. First, you can end the relationship. Second, you and your romantic partner and their spouse can move to another state. In Maryland you might just want to pay the $10 fine. No, we didn't leave off any zeros. As of 2014 an adultery conviction in Maryland results in a ten dollar fine.

It is true that adultery laws are rarely enforced. However, as long as the laws are on the books, your line family would be at risk from anyone who wanted to make trouble for you. Even in "liberal" states and cities there will be people who do not approve of your living situation. A person wanting to harass your family can make a complaint based on a law that is still in the statutes, even if that law is seldom used.

Cohabitation Agreements

For unmarried cohabitating couples, you can choose to define your relationship in writing, instead of letting the state define it for you. Look into creating a cohabitation agreement. Do not mention sex, romance or intimacy as the states all define intimacy as something sexual. (Send your state representative a copy of this book so that they can learn the broader definitions of intimacy.)

Cohabitation describes a type of relationship between two unmarried people. It used to matter in some states if the people involved are the same sex or not. Other states such as Washington, recognize same sex cohabitation. In all the state laws we have looked at, the term cohabitation refers to couples when referring to an adult relationship. The main features of cohabitation are that the individuals live together, share a romantic or intimate relationship and hold themselves out as married. That means you tell people that you are spouses, call each other husband or wife or you use the same last name. These are some of the same types of tests used in common-law-marriage states.

We looked for state definitions of a "sexual relationship" but found nothing specific in state laws. We found plenty of specific definitions of sexual contact, but not relationship. We eventually found a website that gave us some answers, http://definitions.uslegal.com/s/sexual-relations/. According to this website the term "sexual relations" does not necessarily mean penetrative intercourse. It can mean simply touching another person's "private parts."

Like marriage, a cohabitation agreement is a legal contract that is reportedly recognized in 48 of the 50 states as of May 2014. Our source for the number of states recognizing cohabitation agreements is Natalie T. Lorenz and her 2012 article "Cohabitation Agreements after the Civil Union Act." Found at http://www.isba. org/ibj/2012/06/ cohabitationagreementsafterthecivil. Ms. Lorenz states, "The Civil Union Act represents a movement away from Illinois' public policy of encouraging only traditional heterosexual married couple relationships, prompting the question: Should Illinois join 47 other states and recognize unmarried couples' cohabitation agreements, too?" A good question because as of 9/9/2014 Illinois has a law on the books making it illegal for unmarried adults to engage in consensual sexual activity (720 ILCS 5/11-40) was (720 ILCS 5/11-8).

One of our consulting attorneys tells us that cohabitation agreements have value even in a state that does not recognize such agreements as valid contracts. A person's memory is subject to modification and suggestion. Having details about property, finances and responsibilities helps avoid confusion and disagreements later on. For the same reasons we feel that cohabitation agreements for a poly family are of value even though no state would likely recognize them as legal contracts.

A typical cohabitation agreement will cover specific financial issues such as shared and individual expenses and describe separate and communal property. If the relationship ends, the agreement can specify who is responsible for both short- and long-term debts. The cohabitation agreement – in a state where it is recognized – can also be used to pass on personal possessions, money and real property in the event of death. However, we recommend that you consider trusts for estate planning. (See Chapter 5, Finances for more details about trusts.)

When a relationship ends under a cohabitation agreement, each individual is usually entitled to their own personal property, monies and individually held real property. Furthermore, courts usually do not award financial support to either partner. That means that neither partner is required to pay for the support of a former partner to whom they were not married. Each person is solely responsible for debts created in their own name.

Like wills and trusts, cohabitation agreements must meet a few requirements to be considered a valid document. The American Bar Association has a list of recommendations, on its website, for cohabitation agreements. Find the link at www.line-family.info/CALF_companion/ (it is extremely long). Following is a modification of the list that we think might be applicable to members of a polyamorous family. This is not legal advice; it is just our best guess of the basics you might want to consider. Your mileage may vary. You do not need to use "legalese" in writing your cohabitation agreements. However, we recommend that you have your attorney check over your agreement before signing and notarizing it.

A statement of purpose is a good idea. This will be different from a couple's agreement. Your purpose will be to identify your relationship with the family. You might also want to state that you understand that this is a legally binding document (even if it isn't at the moment). It gives an indication of the intent of all parties. If the family moves (or expands) to another state, check the laws to make sure that you are complying as closely as you can with that state's statutes. Also be aware that in your state, the law may change.

For this example we are going to assume that you will have a cohabitation agreement with each of your adult family partners because current laws only recognize agreements between two people. For a family of 4 adults there would be 6 separate cohabitation agreements. A family of 5 would generate 10 agreements. You should state the legal name of one of your partners in each agreement. You must also identify yourself. We wouldn't suggest using your social security number. Instead you might consider using driver's license numbers or state identity card numbers for self-identification. Other information you could use is the age, place of birth and passport numbers for both parties.

It is a good idea for each person to attach a detailed list of personal and real property and debts such as car payments or mortgages. Perhaps you want to include a statement that any debts incurred by an individual will be that individual's responsibility. An individual's personal property and money should be clearly identified as such. Disclosing current wills and trusts helps to keep everyone's intentions clear in case of death or incapacitation.

A new member's financial commitment to become a full partner in the family real estate, if any, should be clear and detailed. It's not like community property laws apply to polyamorous families. The methods for paying a financial obligation to the family could be outlined in the agreement. Two options are immediate full payment or periodic payments until real estate partnership level is reached. If a new family member has valuable professional skills as a carpenter, doctor, lawyer, etc. it would be good to note how those skills - used for the family - would be applied to their financial obligations.

Provide details about monthly and annual family expenses. Describe what fixed expenses need to be covered each month. This would include things such as grocery staples, utility bills, internet connection, insurance, etc. Also describe how irregular expenses are handled. That could include reserve-account funding for things such as building maintenance and repair, vehicle repair, parties, education for children and adults, etc. (see Chapter 5, Finances).

Spell out the rights and responsibilities of the parties to the cohabitation agreement as specifically as possible. This should not limit or restrict a family member's ability to grow and change how they interact with the family. We feel that some important items to describe, in addition to financial obligations, are the expected labor contributions and involvement in family management.

Like the family vision document, cohabitation agreements should have a process in place for review and renegotiation. Describe provisions for modifying the agreement. Remember that change is the only universal constant.

Include promises from each party to the agreements to provide something of value to the other person. This will help increase the potential validity of the cohabitation agreements. These things of value can vary greatly. Some examples are babysitting, tutoring, professional skills, craft skills, doing a share of the housework, etc.

Do not mention any type of sexual or intimate relationship as most jurisdictions will probably void the agreement because it will be assumed that you are entering a meretricious relationship. Contracting for sex is rarely, if ever, looked upon with favor by the courts - except for marriage. Many states explicitly tie sex and marriage together. Eleven states have laws on the books making consensual sex between unmarried adults illegal. The states are Florida, Georgia, Idaho, Illinois, Massachusetts, Minnesota, Mississippi, North Carolina, South Carolina, Utah and Virginia. See the state law references at, http://www.line-family.info/CALF_companion/.

Lack of consummation of a marriage is often one test for whether a marriage can be annulled. Annulling a marriage means that the marriage never existed. To be clear that we are talking about sex, here is the definition of consummate:

> con·sum·mate
>
> *verb*
>
> ˈkänsəˌmāt/
>
> 1. make (a marriage or relationship) complete
>   by having sexual intercourse.

While no-fault divorce is in effect in most states, sexual impotency of either partner can be used for grounds for divorce in many states. Following are a few examples:

Alaska - AS 25.24.050

(1) failure to consummate the marriage at the time of the marriage and continuing at the commencement of the action;

Maine - Title 19-A, 902, 1.

B. Impotence;

Mississippi - Title 93, 5, 1

Divorces from the bonds of matrimony may be decreed to the injured party for any one or more of the following twelve (12) causes:

First. Natural impotency.

Rhode Island - Title 15-5-2

(1) Impotency;

Tennessee - Title 36 – 5 – 101

(1) Either party, at the time of the contract, was and still is naturally impotent and incapable of procreation;

Prior to no-fault divorce, impotency as grounds for divorce was nearly universal in the United States. Therefore since marriage is defined as a contract by most states, marriage between two people is the one form of contracting for sex that is currently approved and defined in law.

Who Are a Child's Legal Parents?

Rights and responsibilities for children is an important consideration. Legal parents have the primary legal responsibility for their children. A child can have three legal parents in Louisiana, Delaware, Pennsylvania, D.C., Oregon, Washington, Massachusetts and Alaska if a surrogate was involved in the birth of the child. In California the number of legal parents is unlimited. To gain legal parent status for an unrelated adult in California takes the declaration of a judge. The legal parents can be either biological or adoptive. Blood relatives in and out of the line family and adults with whom a child has developed an emotional attachment can have a role in the child's life. However, they have no parental rights where the child is concerned unless a court has made a legal declaration that such rights exist.

If you are the parent of a child under the age of 18, we strongly urge you to go to Alexis Neely's website http://kidsprotectionplan.com/. The site provides a free child-guardian agreement for legal parents to fill out. This agreement protects your children from being taken into protective custody by the state in case of your death, incapacitation or incarceration. A custody transfer plan also keeps your child from going to relatives who you feel are not fit to be your children's parents. Check out Chapter 6, Children for more details.

Growing Apart – Planning for Breakups

Usually the purpose of creating a polyamorous family is to produce an environment that supports and encourages long-term relationships. However things can change for an individual. Details regarding a person ending their relationship with the family and leaving should be addressed in the cohabitation agreement. It has also been suggested by an attorney that you include a statement like, "We agree that polyamory is a non-issue in the event of relationship breakdown." We have seen polyamory used as a weapon in divorce proceedings. If planning for a possible relationship breakdown is not in place, the family could be subject to costly and time-consuming litigation. Separate legal counsel for each party is needed in this case. It will get expensive. That is why you need to plan ahead.

If a relationship ends, the agreement should specify who is responsible for any debts incurred by the person leaving. If loans were made for the family's benefit, it is likely that the family will assume the responsibility. However, a debt created using family collateral for personal projects would usually be the individual's personal debt.

The departing individual is entitled to their personal property, monies and individually held real property. No one should have to give up personal property or have it counted as part of a dissolution settlement. They need to be given a fair amount of compensation for their financial contribution to the family. In addition, funds from any joint investment group should be paid in relationship to how the fund has grown or shrunk. Periodic payments should be negotiated if a lump-sum compensation would severely hurt the family's finances. The laws we have reviewed state that no party is entitled to financial support in a cohabitation dissolution. Unless plural cohabitation is recognized sometime in the future it is unlikely a judge would grant financial support.

At the bottom of the cohabitation agreement, make sure that it has been signed by both parties named at the top. Signing this document should clearly state that both individuals have signed of their own free will without coercion and that they are not under duress. We have seen the suggestion that a video of the signing process is a good idea for helping to prove it was not a coercive situation. Your family might want to make a ritual out of it. After all, it is an important life decision. We feel it deserves a party.

Postdating the cohabitation agreement might be a good idea. Perhaps a month would be a good "cooling off" period. After spending a lot of time getting to know the family, it will probably be stressful waiting through the family decision-making process of accepting a new member. This could make the applicant overly eager to sign the cohabitation agreement. A period of reflection is a good idea to prove non-coercion and let the prospective member consider the importance of their decision. Fairness, and the appearance of fairness, are important concepts in legal agreements. We think that giving an individual time to reconsider their decision provides an extra measure of fairness.

To our knowledge, cohabitation agreements for more than two people have not been tested in any court of law. However, we feel having them in place is better than not. At the very least your cohabitation agreements will provide clarity of intent and description of rights and responsibilities in your family relationships. In case of relationship dissolution, your cohabitation agreements might provide guidance to an amicable resolution of disputes with a departing family member.

Where do You Want to Live?

We can give you some information about which states might be more (or less) accommodating of a polyamorous family. We have already mentioned the states that have anti-adultery laws. In addition, there are currently laws on the books that make consensual sex between unmarried adults illegal in eleven states. There are laws against unmarried adult cohabitation. There are even laws about the sale or possession of sex toys. It is a good idea to know about these laws. Even if these laws are not enforced, someone can make a complaint as long as the laws exist. Check out a few of the more interesting state laws at: http://www.line-family.info/CALF_companion/.

We are pleased that marriage equality for all couples is now the law in the U.S. thanks to the 5-4 Supreme Court ruling in Obergefill v. Hodges. However, some local jurisdictions are fighting the decision by not issuing any marriage licenses. Another tactic is refusing to process applications for marriage licenses submitted by same-sex couples. They are hoping that one or more of these same-sex couples will sue them. The goal is to get another same-sex marriage case in front of the U.S. Supreme Court. It's not likely the court would revisit the question anytime soon.

Local county, parish and city governments can make life difficult for your family even if the state laws look reasonable. Local laws often limit the number of unrelated adults that can occupy a single dwelling unit. Regular payments to family expense funds might be seen as rent for taxation purposes. These are just two examples. Local laws can cause your family trouble and cost money.

One method of sidestepping a lot of issues with busybody neighbors and local and state authorities is to set up housekeeping far away from neighbors and local authorities. Lots of folks move to the country for the freedom and privacy it offers. Of course moving to the country probably won't work for you if your family's values and vision focuses on things such as cultural events, politics, public service, etc. Please note that we are not advocating breaking any laws. However, you are less likely to get hit with a nuisance complaint if your nearest neighbor is several miles away. Even if you win a nuisance complaint, it still costs you money and time to defend yourself.

Imagine you want to join a polyamorous family that is organized under an LLC. Further, let's say that your state, such as California, Washington and Ohio, defines a limited liability company as a person. Could you have a cohabitation agreement with the family LLC? We don't think so. Just to be clear, corporate personhood was originally created to be a convenient legal fiction that allows a corporate entity to enter into contracts, sue, be sued and pay taxes. However, we would bet that a cohabitation agreement with an LLC would not fly with any judges. However, there is a way to organize a family under an LLC and we will discuss that in the next section.

We have based this chapter on reading state laws, consulting with attorneys and visiting many websites that provide legal opinions. Again we must say that we are not attorneys. We do not provide legal counsel. We have provided some references so that your attorney can see where we got our layman's opinions.

Line Family Cohabitation

Two general concepts can be used for developing cohabitation agreements for a polyamorous family. One would be for you to have a separate agreement with every member of the family. This could create a lot of paperwork. We mentioned that a 4-adult family would need 6 cohabitation agreements and a family of 5 would need 10. A 20-adult line family would require 190 agreements. It may not be all that daunting if managed as computer records. The other option is to define rights and responsibilities of the family members using a legal entity such as an LLC or a corporate structure.

First let's consider the multiple cohabitation agreements concept. Would a line family's (or poly family's) set of cohabitation agreements be upheld in a court of law? As we have said, we don't know but we don't think so. But laws sometimes change when they are challenged. What the cohabitation agreements will do is help to clarify the rights and responsibilities of the family and its individual members. Hopefully it will be a long time before anyone has a need to take their paperwork to court.

However, all of the rules and references we have seen regarding cohabitation agreements refer to couples. This makes sense within the current legal frameworks of all 50 states. The only laws we have found dealing with conjugal relationships of three or more people are the bigamy, adultery and polygamy statutes (none of which are friendly to non-monogamous, non-exclusive relationships).

A Viable Legal Framework for Your Line Family

We spoke with an attorney, who is familiar with the line family concept, about the question of how cohabitation by three or more people could be handled under existing law. He understood what we are trying to do because he had read Heinlein's The Moon is a Harsh Mistress. He had already worked out how a non-bloodline, multigenerational family might use the laws in Washington State to organize and manage the family and its holdings.

Note: In this section we will be using the laws of Washington State extensively in our example. Washington State is where we currently live. More importantly, the lawyer we talked to is licensed to practice law in Washington State. We think that this example might translate fairly well to most other states but that's for local attorneys where you live to figure out. You might want to look at this book's support website, www. line-family.info/CALF_companion/ for a review of laws on the books in various states.

To form a line family, the attorney we spoke with would rely on a legal entity such as a limited liability company (LLC) or a corporate model. Line family member's co-ownership and cohabitation could be governed by one of those legal entities. That means you would be sharing equity and ownership of line family assets as a member of an LLC or corporation. These structures allow you to add or remove people without needing to change a list of names on titles and deeds to family property. All you are doing is adding or subtracting members of the governing LLC or the corporate shareholders of the line family.

Given a choice between an LLC or corporate governing entity, we would opt for an LLC. Our main reason for this choice is the current fact that LLCs are not subject to federal income tax. Income generated by the LLC passes directly through to the owners of the LLC. Corporations, on the other hand, are usually taxed on their income in addition to taxing the shareholder's income. Also, there can be extra privacy with an LLC because there is often no official board of directors required like there is for corporations. Corporate board meetings must have minutes recorded. Any notes or meeting minutes of an LLC are voluntary and private as long as the operating agreement is written so that, "...the certificate of formation and limited liability company agreement do not expressly require the holding of meetings of members or managers." (RCW 25.15.060). It's your choice.

LLCs also have the option of being classified as a partnership, a C corporation or an S corporation (see IRS Pub. 3402, Taxation of LLCs). Your choice would depend on how your LLC operates and what would give you the greatest tax advantage. As a partnership, each partner owns a percentage of the LLC's assets for federal income tax purposes. LLCs do pay taxes on things such as wages for employees. IRS Pub. 3402 states,

"If it is an S corporation, the corporation is generally not subject to any income tax and the income deductions, gains, losses and credits of the corporation 'pass through' to the members." We strongly urge you to find an attorney to help you set up your LLC in a way that best serves your needs.

LLCs can provide an overall framework for managing a line family. It is done with the operating agreement. The agreement describing membership in the LLC might have many of the elements found in a couple's cohabitation agreement. We listed several suggested topics earlier in this chapter. Specifics in the operating agreement could include:

1. a statement of purpose,
2. a new member's financial commitment to become a full member,
3. a description of monthly and annual LLC expenses and reserve accounts,
4. involvement in LLC management,
5. how dissolution payments are made to a departing LLC member, and
6. minimum labor requirements for property maintenance and upkeep.

You will probably want to include a statement about how your operating agreement can be amended. This might include the type of decision-making process to use, time frame for a proposed amendment to be acted on and anything else that seems appropriate. Another question is if you want only fully vested (paid) line family members to be able to decide the fate of a proposed amendment to the operating agreement. Would you allow new, less vested, members to vote or only participate in the discussion? Make sure this is clear in the initial operating agreement.

Other topics found in a couple's cohabitation agreement might be handled in a separate document that is kept on file with other private line family records. These files would contain information about each new member as they joined the family. This could include a list of an individual's separate property both real and personal including debts, investment accounts, land, etc.

On the issue of privacy, an LLC can be the beneficiary of a trust – including a land trust. An LLC would add a layer of privacy to the family's primary residence, but it would also add a layer of cost. For more details, see our discussion of owning primary residential real estate with an LLC in Chapter 8, Owning Real Property. Also in Chapter 8, we talk about the privacy and flexibility of putting the family's primary residential real estate in a land trust. It is something to seriously consider. An LLC can be a good governing entity for your line family businesses. Trusts can be used to manage other family assets such as investment accounts, vehicles, powered machinery, etc. Anything of significant value can be put into a trust. To save some money spent on professional trustees, two of your respected family members could act as trustees. Be sure you have alternate trustees named in case the primary trustees choose to retire or are not able to carry out their responsibilities.

What should not be in an LLC operating agreement? As in a cohabitation agreement, you want to avoid talking about anything that could be interpreted as a romantic or sexual contract. That can get a couple's cohabitation agreement nullified quickly. Imagine the reaction of a judge to anything the least bit sexual that included more than two people in your operating agreement.

An operating agreement, trust or any document involving land should avoid restrictions on the sale of any real estate owned or controlled by the family. The practical reason is that your family might decide to move at some time in the future. The other reason is that you can't restrict the sale of real estate forever because it violates "Dead Hand" provisions in the law. The family real estate can stay in the line family forever because land trusts and LLCs can exist in perpetuity. But the potential to sell the land must exist.

The attorney told us that in using these business documents you're fudging a relationship and blurring the lines between business and interpersonal relationships. We don't think it is too different from a marriage. State laws that we looked at kept referring to marriage as a contract and contracts are about exchanging value for value. Marriage is something that joins two people's incomes and properties into some kind of cooperative relationship.

In Washington State all you need to do to get married is be old enough, not too closely related to each other by blood and not already be married to anyone else. You do not need a ceremony. All you need is a license, a couple of witnesses, a person who is authorized to perform marriages and a pen to sign the marriage certificate. Everything else is optional. While it's true that we are talking about using business models that were created for managing profit to manage interpersonal relationships, how different is it from a marriage? You are doing essentially the same thing for more than two people when using a business entity to set up a cooperative relationship. Using business entities to define personal relationships is a somewhat new idea. However, the attorney said that, "It's not so big of a stretch that the law can't stretch to accommodate it."

Elon's Opinion on Cohabitation Arrangements

I'm certainly in favor of cohabitation! And I can see a need for agreements about that - especially for a line family. I'll admit that I balked at the idea of having one agreement for every two people though! It's like the Costco Warehouse version. Richard explained to me that for there to be any chance of the agreements standing up in court - should things happen to go that badly - then the agreement had better be between 2 people, not 20. Ok, I get that. My suggestion is that you write the agreements so carefully, and lovingly, that the act of writing them, and later reviewing them, will help to hold your family together. And that the clarity with which the agreements are written will assist in resolving any issues that come up if someone decides to leave, or is asked to leave. Group hug!

CHAPTER TWELVE

The Windward Line Family

To make music is the essential thing – to listen to it is accessory.

Charles Seeger

As we crawled our way up the alternately paved and rough gravel road we were glad we were in our jeep. The road was not rutted, washed out or otherwise deteriorating. It was just bad enough to keep casual drivers from venturing too far. The instructions were difficult to follow, but they eventually got us to the Windward property. We were there for a long weekend of classes and presentations at the Windward Education & Research Center. The core members are a line family with property in south central Washington State.

We learned about Windward while searching the web for any information we could find about line families. We had been using the search term "line marriage" and found a lot of Robert Heinlein references. Not a big surprise. Richard liked the term "line family" much better. One day he tried a search of that term expecting nothing. What he got was a link to the Windward website. Exploring the website we found out about some of their work in renewable energy, sustainable food production, energy efficient construction and other rural-living projects they are actively pursuing.

A visit to Windward seemed like a good idea. Fortunately they were having an open house/educational weekend and we signed up. After arriving and finding a suitable campsite, we started to pitch the tent. It was Elon's tent and Richard had never set it up, therefore she was directing the pitching of the tent. That is when we first met Walt, the senior member of the line family and the only remaining founder of Windward. As Elon was busy telling Richard how things went together, Walt caught Richard's attention and said with a smile, "I see you like uppity women too." We knew we were going to like him.

In this chapter you will read quotes from the four members of the of the Windward line family. We have already mentioned Walt. We also received comments from Lindsay, Andrew and Opalyn. Ruben, a Steward at Windward, describes how his life is affected by living in a rural area. Each one has their own perspective on what Windward is about, but they share an overall vision of a sustainable lifestyle. They have a commitment to educating others about what they have learned. They are also open to learning from their visitors.

Levels of Involvement with Windward

As the weekend progressed we learned that there are different levels of involvement in life at Windward. At the core is the line family, comprised of individuals who have committed themselves to being the main caretakers of the land and the community that supports their vision. Other types of involvement include:

Stewards, who have not yet decided whether they desire to become members of the line family. Stewards can pursue special interests rather than the general whole-system focus expected of members of the line family.

Assistant Stewards, who are working through the two-year process that leads to becoming recognized as a Steward.

Apprentices, who come to study a specific skill or practice, such as forest-based permaculture, sustainable animal husbandry, representative consensus or non-patriarchal social structures.

Interns, who come to gain a sense of what living in a land-based intentional community involves.

Academic Fellows, who come to use Windward as a living laboratory in conjunction with an academic program that requires them to do field work.

The Away Team, is comprised of individuals who do not live at Windward full time but who are supportive of Windward's broad goals.

A reading list with web links is posted on the Windward website for folks looking to study, and perhaps follow, alternative paths described in the books. One book on the list is "*Cradle to Cradle: Remaking the Way We Make Things*", by McDonough and Braungart. The authors challenge the "Recycle" portion of the slogan "Reduce, Reuse, Recycle" as merely slowing the industrial revolution's cradle to grave manufacturing model. Recycling generally means that materials will be reused in a lower quality form before finally ending up in a landfill. The authors contend that materials can be up-cycled into higher quality uses and mimic biological systems that use waste as food for new processes.

Other books on their list include: "*Solvia, A Safe and Sustainable World*", "*Forgotten Founders*", "*Work and Worship Among the Shakers*", "*Without Sin: The Life and Death of the Oneida Community*", "*The Moon is a Harsh Mistress*", "*Looking Backward*", "*Herland*", "*Radical Evolution*", and "*Pillars of the Earth.*" Find the list at, (http://www.windward.org/internship/book6701.htm).

In addition to the list of books there is a collection of essays and editorials by members of the Windward community. They give an insight into life at Windward, the kinds of work that is being done and plans for future projects. If you are interested in participating at Windward, being prepared and passionate will earn you lots of points when decisions are made about who to invite to share in the Windward experience. Windward's website can be found at, http://www.windward.org/2.0 / index.php.

For a less strenuous and more peripheral involvement with Windward, you could become:

A True Fan, and directly support the open-source research Windward is doing in developing a process for the conversion of woody biomass into vehicular fuel at a village scale. 'The Biomass2Methanol project aims to model a holistic, forest-based energy economy that converts forest material into the diverse forms of energy needed to empower rural communities while maintaining healthy forests.

A Participant in open house events such as the Village Helix held around the 4th of July weekend each year.

And last, but not least, authors who writes chapters about them in a book.

Windward's History and Focus on Sustainability

As of 2015, Windward has existed as a line family for well over 30 years. Currently the line family is fairly small, only 4 people—two women (Opalyn and Lindsay) and two men (Walt and Andrew). Their ages range from 24 to 64. The line family has been larger in the past, but life happens – some died and others had a change of dreams. They do attract a good number of interns and other people with varying levels of involvement. We feel their success is amazing considering they had no role models to follow, no books to give them advice and no societal support.

Lindsay discusses the vision and goals of Windward.

Windward's focus is on developing a culture that can survive and thrive within the bounds of the natural world. This includes developing and maintaining a diverse body of knowledge, skills and practices that enable us to both live well with the land and with one another. As a line family, we acknowledge that there is no authority higher than Nature and consider stewardship of the land and the people that tend it integral to our success. Within this framework, we encourage individuals to develop their own areas of interest as well as to pursue personal spiritual and creative practices.

Walt describes Windward's land.

Windward's property is described by Walt as a dry marginal forest, therefore the land was relatively inexpensive. He feels that if they can create a viable life-support network on marginal land, the techniques they develop will certainly work on richer and more fertile land. Walt explains why owning land is important in the formation of a community.

The dream of community generally transforms into a reality when land is purchased because without a land base, a community is highly unlikely to last. It's not just a matter of the economics that come with owning the land on which you live and upon which you make your living. There's something visceral in becoming bonded to a place. It provides a sense of belonging and continuity that can't be achieved by renting someone else's land.

But that leads to a host of questions such as, 'Where is the capital to buy the land going to come from, and who's going to own the land once it's paid for?' In Windward's case, we traded time for money and paid for the land on ten year contracts instead of 30 year mortgages. Since the majority of our income went to land payments, this made us 'land poor'. But by accelerating the payment rate, we kept the total amount of interest paid low and eventually got to the place where the contracts were paid off. During that time, we were not able to fund the construction projects we would have liked to, but we did what we could without going into debt. One of the profound achievements of the older members of the line was to pass along our most central tangible asset--the land-- to the new members debt free.

When we went looking for land in the mid-80's, a key strategy was to not look for land that was in high demand because it had lots of commercial potential. By going off the beaten path, we were able to acquire 131 acres of forest and pasture sufficient to enable us to have a reasonable chance of feeding, clothing and fueling twenty people using sustainable land practices. Land with better access and more water would have cost a lot more, would have taken a lot longer to pay off, would have cost more in taxes and would have been more difficult to develop because of tighter zoning issues.

Owning land that is more commercial can also destroy a community by tempting community leaders to shut down the community, sell off the land and pocket the money. Communities in which the land is owned by a founding couple often crash when the founders' marriage crashes and the land has to be sold in order to settle the divorce. A line family's legal form can be that of a non-profit corporation, in which case the decision of a member to withdraw doesn't force the remaining members to buy them out, thereby helping to ensure the perpetuity of the line for those who still want to go forward.

During the open house, various family members and interns showed us the projects that they were involved with. As a conservation and renewable energy activist of the 70s and early 80s, Richard was extremely interested in Windward's advances in seasonal solar heating systems, waste wood fuel generation and small scale aquaponics systems.

Walt's explanation of aquaponics.

Aquaponics is a technology that uses fish waste to fertilize edible plants grown in a closed water-cycling system. At the same time, those plants purify the water used to grow edible fish. This work is key to enabling the production of both vegetable and protein for groups that have to work with limited amounts of land and water.

––––––––––––

Windward is working to develop more efficient aquaponics systems that will work with a single family dwelling unit of 2 to 4 people, as well as larger systems that can help supply fresh vegetables, fruits and fish for a community of 15 to 20 people.

Windward also uses grey-water to grow non-edible plants such as lavender. Grey-water is what is left over when you have done laundry, washed dishes or washed your hands. It is generally best to use biodegradable soap when using grey-water for aquaponics. Water that comes from the old technology of flush toilets is called black-water. You cannot use black-water in aquaponics or to water gardens.

Lindsay describes food production at Windward.

Windward is a working farm with livestock including chickens, ducks, rabbits, goats, sheep and pigs. Between the garden and the animals, a large amount of Windward's food is produced on site and is supplemented with food grown regionally. Lindsay explains how food production and eating is more than simple nutrition.

Eating is a very intimate act. How I choose to nourish my body, how I relate to the land, people, animals, plants and processes that have created the food that I am literally incorporating into my own being is an indicator of how I choose to relate to the world around me. Living closely with animals, understanding their nature, listening to their needs, seeing our own emotions reflected back at us through their demeanor, helps us become more human. It helps us better understand ourselves and helps us to recognize our own animal nature. Sharing our lives closely with animals is humbling, deeply grounding and it can help us internalize that we too are governed by the laws of nature, that we too are mortal. Our capacity to create a life in balance with the natural world, that so many now are realizing is necessary to our survival as a nation, a global society and a human community, depends on this kind of deep transformation.

As a vegetarian for 15 years, during 10 of which I was a vegan, I never thought that I would come to a place in myself where I deeply understood that the best way I could honor the life of an animal whom I loved and who offered so much to me would be to incorporate that animal's body into my own. But I am in that place now. It's this kind of real, tangible connection to the systems, creatures and elements that enable us to live that allows for the internal shifts necessary to think beyond the self and understand our place in the greater context.

If you are squeamish about where meat comes from, this might not be the place for you. Windward welcomes both vegetarians and omnivores. Family members consider what you eat to be a personal choice. The choice to eat meat is very personal at Windward as you can experience the whole process and take responsibility for your choices. If you have seen the movie "Food Inc." you will understand that Windward's animals have a good life.

Andrew discusses his role in providing a good life for the livestock.

I came to Windward as a vegetarian of almost 10 years. I'd decided long ago that I would not support the anonymous, industrial methods of animal husbandry. I believed that unless I could have a stake in the well-being of the animal, and could then bring myself to take the life of that animal, I could not honorably (or ethically) eat the animal.

I am the primary caretaker of Windward's herd of sheep and goats, from birth to death. I live a rich and rewarding life with them. I know them as friends and colleagues, each and every one with their own personality.

With the initial guidance of Walt, I am now the primary person who handles the harvesting of all the animals we eat as food. The process of being able to give the animals a good death is as much a part of my role as a caretaker as my capacity to give them a good life.

Oddly enough, these animals are some of my greatest teachers because they are experts at reading body language, and thus our unconscious mental states. If I am in a sullen mood, I am often greeted by the goats with a supportive bleat, as if they are asking 'what's the matter dear'. If I happen to be agitated, my jerky motions can make the chickens apprehensive to come near me. This dynamic has been a constant source of material for self-reflection, something which I cherish greatly.

One of my greatest pleasures with regard to working with animals is to design systems which simultaneously improve the quality of the land and its capacity to support people and animals, while also giving the animals meaningful work to do that is well suited to their natural tendencies. Whether it is goats de-foliating branches from forest thinning, or pigs tilling up earth before planting perennial pasture, the animals contribute much to our life and I enjoy the pleasure of working closely with them.

————————————

Consumerism is a one-way street upon which industrialized societies have based their economies. But even the longest one-way street comes to an end. Call it peak oil, climate change or overpopulation, the street will end and everyone will suffer. Windward residents call what they are creating a "post-consumer village."

Walt describes the inevitable collapse of a consumer system based on non-renewable resources.

As the age of abundant non-renewable resources draws to an end, people will need to work out ways to produce locally the resources they need in sustainable ways. This involves a radical restructuring of how people live with each other, with the land that sustains them and the technology they use to improve their lives.

As the consumer system becomes ever less reliable, people will need to transition from being consumers to being producers, learning how to use local resources wisely to meet their needs and to generate the goods they will need to trade for the things they don't produce. We see the transition from the urban/suburban way of living to a land based way of life as a return to the fundamentals, and so we study ways to light and heat our homes that do not rely on steady inputs of ever scarcer resources. We're focusing on how to integrate into the landscape the production of the materials needed to sustain a village using methods such as food forests to grow food, forage, fiber and biomass.

The more efficient such a village is, the more sustainable it will be, and the better role model it can be for others who also yearn to be free of the system. Our goal is to show a way that people can return to the path of stewarding the land and each other's welfare. The work is too large to be done alone, which is why we feel that organizational structures larger than the nuclear family are necessary.

Financial and Work Requirements at Windward

Windward's members consider themselves self-reliant, but money is still needed for the necessities and niceties that cannot be provided directly from the land. Therefore everyone living on the Windward property is expected to contribute $400 a month while they live there.

Even if they were totally self-sufficient and off the grid, there are chores that need to be done. While living at Windward everyone must work at least 2 hours a day, 6 days a week on operational systems such as feeding the animals, watering the garden or cooking lunch. This is quite a bit less than any intentional community we have visited or read about. The fact is everyone puts in more than 2 hours a day, the additional time going primarily to the projects the individual feels are most meaningful to them personally.

Opalyn compares working for someone else and working with your community.

Working together to meet our core needs for food, shelter and energy frees us up to work on the projects we take joy in. Most people spend a significant part of their day working unfulfilling jobs in order to pay their debts with very little time left over for themselves. By working with and for each other, we're able to enjoy an enhanced quality of life and also have time to do meaningful things. By tailoring our efforts on behalf of the community to focus on the things we do especially well or especially enjoy doing, we're able to increase our perception that we are well-rewarded for pulling our own weight.

No matter what project they take on, the folks who live at Windward are passionate about what they are doing and bring a sense of dedication and drive to their chosen tasks. Occasionally this can lead to an individual generating income from goods that they produce. These individual enterprises are encouraged. The closest Windward gets to having a family business are the events that they hold or sponsor on their property.

Walt explains some of the thinking behind not creating Windward family businesses.

One reason why Windward does not operate an

organizational business is out of a desire to ensure that the organization serves its members, rather than the other way around. We've all had experience with the employer/employee dynamic and do not want that brought into our home. One result is that we have a strong desire to see each of our members become financially independent in ways that align with their talents and long term interests. Often that involves each person engaging in a handful of economic enterprises to create what we call their 'income quilt'.

Ruben shares some of his experiences creating his income quilt.

After deciding to take on a life at Windward, I had to answer the more practical question of how to make this undertaking financially viable. I eventually decided to join the local workforce, which is a challenging choice given the remote location of Windward and the generally depressed economy of rural areas, but also an opportunity since employers have a very limited labor pool to select from and often struggle to find quality personnel.

The community helped me in this endeavor by facilitating my taking courses at the community college to become a certified nursing aide (CNA). I now work part time, two 12 hour shifts a week, at the local hospital. This job allows me to move between worlds, to support Windward and work on projects that excite me while I'm on site, and to connect and serve the larger regional community as a loyal member of the local hospital staff. For me this is the ideal arrangement, as the two social scenes complement each other nicely, and I get to have meaningful relationships and do meaningful work in every area of my life.

Being part of Windward actually made finding a job easier. If I was living in the city, I would have to have a full time job in order to rent an apartment and pay the higher costs associated with living alone. Because my cost of living is much lower here, I can afford to work part time, and there are lots more part-time jobs out there than there are full-time jobs.

Windward is a seven-days-a-week way of life. The standard Monday through Friday work week doesn't apply since the garden needs watering, the sheep need feeding and the goats need milking regardless of what particular day of the week it is. As a result, it's no hardship for me to work at the hospital on the days that other people want off. The result is that I'm an especially useful employee for the hospital to have since my flexibility enables them to use me to fill in their work schedule so that their full-time employees can take off the days they want. That's good for the hospital, for my fellow workers and for me.

Windward Member's Businesses

Many communities such as Twin Oaks or East Wind have community businesses. As mentioned earlier Windward does not operate a family business. Their attitude about monetary egalitarianism is different from the classic income-sharing concept found in many intentional communities. Instead, Windward sees itself as an expense-sharing cooperative. Walt makes a distinction between opportunity, results, and personal fulfillment.

A community can be focused on ensuring equality of opportunity or equality of result, but not both. We see each person as an individual with different interests, desires and abilities, not as workers on an assembly line. What matters most to us is ensuring that each person has an enhanced opportunity to fulfill their goals within the community; we believe that if we enable that to happen, people will feel more fulfilled. We know that what will please one person very much may not fulfill another at all, so focusing too closely on ensuring that everyone gets or does the same thing is counterproductive. And not only is a difference in ability and desire okay, it's actually an essential part of enabling a community to function sustainably--we see this embracing of diversity as another aspect of our community's poly nature.

The experience of other communities has demonstrated that an excessive focus on making sure that each person does the exact same amount and type of work and receives the exact same amount of compensation is futile and breeds envy and distrust. We'd rather keep the list of core needs short so that we can focus our energy on the things that bring us joy.

Windward's focus on creating opportunity means that individuals can use the community's land, tools and technologies to develop their own businesses. For example, one person uses garden space to grow herbs and garlic for her business. Another person is working to turn waste wood into liquid fuel. If a person develops a business and makes lots of money, they are still only required to contribute $400 a month to live on the property. The balance of their income is theirs to do with as they will.

Lindsay defines the word "economy" and how it relates to a community.

We are working to create our own internal economy to meet our needs and desires. The word 'economy' comes from

combining the Greek word for home or household, *oikos,* with
the act of stewarding or managing, *nomos (e.g. oiko-nomos).* So
when I say we are creating our own economy, I mean we are
collectively stewarding and providing for our own household
and home so that we are not dependent on the global economic
system to provide for us.

Designing a Community Economy

Opalyn explains how their economy can be used to provide benefit for
the individual members of Windward while improving the infrastructure
and value of the community. In addition, she is learning skills that the
community can use in the future. It is an impressive return on every
dollar invested.

Most people spend a considerable amount of time
working to make their rent or mortgage payments, activities
which do a lot to enrich the landlords and bankers, but not so
much to empower the people doing the work. As an expense-
sharing cooperative, we're able to 'pay ourselves', which allows
the cooperative to accumulate land, buildings and infrastructure.
The structures we build and the food we grow meet our needs,
not those of the consumer economy. Because we do this work
ourselves and for ourselves, it's really rather liberating. The
difference is akin to between being ill used by the system and
being well used on behalf of one's beloved.

For example, how many landlords would allow me to use
half of my monthly rent to build my own place? Not very many.
But this is one way to think of what I am doing at Windward. I
contribute $400 per month like everyone else, and I spend up to
$200 of my monthly contribution on materials to build a home

that's custom tailored to suit my basic needs. I am well into the process of converting a 40-foot long shipping container into a 300 square foot apartment. Some might exclaim, '300 square feet? Isn't that pretty small?' Well, yes! But when I have a wide range of separate facilities such as a laundry, a main kitchen, and a variety of work spaces, then 300 SF is plenty, and far easier to maintain. The cost of building materials do add up, but I am pleasantly surprised at how far $200 can go if spent wisely.

I enjoy doing this work at my own pace, and I have plenty of help when needed. I'm learning as I go, so a lot of time is spent reading up on various aspects of the work. I'm not only getting a nice place to stay out of my efforts, I'm gaining a lot of satisfaction in the process. My skills are steadily increasing to the point where I'll soon feel competent to build something larger and more complex. For me, phrases like 'make your bed' have taken on a whole new meaning.

It is likely that the family would see benefit from individual successes. If, for example Windward herbs become a highly valued commodity because of their quality and organic production, it is possible that increased demand might result in additional construction such as a greenhouse with a supporting aquaponics system. Such construction would be financed and done by the individual(s) operating that business.

Walt offers an example of an individual's business benefiting Windward's kitchen.

Take the garlic growing business as an example. Garlic is well suited to Windward's wet springs and dry summers, and one member of the line family earns income by growing organic garlic for sale in markets where they pay top dollar for the largest bulbs. Because not all the garlic grown will meet market standard, Windward's kitchen is well supplied with bulbs that aren't as large or as pretty as the bulbs that do go to market. The steady development of more garlic beds increases Windward's long-term food growing capacity since those additional beds could be repurposed as grow beds for production of vegetables for the family in times of need.

Polyamory – a Windward Perspective

Along with all the sustainable food, energy and housing, the Windward line family also wants to build sustainable relationships. In Walt's words,
…perhaps the greatest challenge we have to address as a community lies in the area of building sustainable relationships. The future is uncertain, but history shows pretty clearly that in hard times the best thing to hold on to is each other.

Lindsay lays out core values for a multi-generational and sustainable community.

We are trying to create a model for a new, and hopefully better, way of living. While in some ways so simple, this task is incredibly complex, nuanced and I believe worthy of our fullest efforts. Towards this end, we relate to the land as our home, community and life-support system, we function within the context of a non-profit organizational entity, we use the line family as a means to carry through time this culture and way of life, and we use our love, sex and intimacy to create and deepen the bonds needed to enable a community to survive, thrive and do meaningful, creative work in the world.

Nothing short of a life-long love affair with this Earth, with the nook of the world we call our home and the people with whom we share it, will produce a culture that can be, and is indeed worth being, sustained. In other words, creating the space in our hearts and the practice in our lives to love inclusively, to care for the well-being of the whole, and to share intimacy, connection and love with multiple people and entities is at the root of living a life in balance with the natural world.

Many call this practice of loving multiple people polyamory. We do too. But more, we recognize that our capacity to love, our sexual energy, and our deep desire for intimacy - for knowing and for being known - are perhaps our most powerful resources. Human connection can inspire and fuel a transition to a new way of living. Actually, I think it's the only thing powerful enough and with enough regenerative force to do so. Human connection can finance the construction of villages, it can provide the ongoing labor needed to tend to living systems, it can channel physical, creative, intellectual, spiritual and erotic energy towards creating a better world. And it's something that is innately fulfilling. It's a win-win.

I like to think of the line family as a tribe of lovers. The transition to a sustainable culture requires a team, a tribe, working collaboratively towards this common goal. No one person could do it alone, nor a couple, nor a nuclear family. While our line family is currently a small tribe, our structure and our willingness to embrace, as whole people, those that share our common values enable us to expand our team in ways that traditional family structures do not.

Integral to the line family and to Windward generally is the *comadre*-- a circle of women that mutually support one another and together create the social context that enables a tribe of lovers to be sustained. In our modern culture, women are taught to consider other women as competition and this encourages a war everlasting for the men worthy of our love. However, when women are able to bond together and trust one another as time-tested allies, when we are able to rely on one another to hold us and to hold us accountable, when we understand that we are more safe, more secure and more loved when we work together to create our home, then we are able to share our love more freely and more fully.

Such confidence in one another enables women to create, or tolerate nothing less than, a culture with an abundance of intimate connections, that accumulates and protects capital, and that is safe and secure for children--leaving behind the patriarchal and consumer paradigm where intimate connection, resource preservation and real security are all scarce. Such a circle of women, aided by the men they love, are able to nurture into existence a culture that is life-affirming and peaceful-- a culture where children are free to run and play, people are free to love and create and this earth is free to continue in its ancient effort of living.

Maintaining trust, respect, affirmation, and good communication between the women, particularly the women of different generations, is perhaps the single most important part of creating a successful, long-term polyamorous line family. When the integrity of this circle of women is maintained, there is little that cannot be accomplished.

Generational Transition

With only one original founder still at Windward, the transition from one generation to the next is almost complete. Being able to acquire the necessary assets to establish a line family is essential. But being able to pass along the assets, skills and knowledge gained to younger people who can sustain the momentum and build continuity is the true test of the potential longevity of a line family. The generation following the founders can dismantle what has been created, change the focus of the family or maintain the vision of the founders. It's a test of character for one generation to hand off the fruits of its labors to another generation. It is a huge test of character for that new generation to step up to the challenge with courage and commitment.

Andrew sees a sustainable future uniting proven concepts and new ideas.

Andrew looks to the future knowing that in combining old and new technologies and social structures that Windward is creating something new and exciting.

Because we are essentially imagineering a new kind of culture, most of the situations we find ourselves in are unprecedented. Just about everything we do is precedent setting, as the decisions we make today will in large part be the standards by which future members will assess whether certain actions or decisions are appropriate.

As a second generation member of the Line, I regard, as a part of my life-work, to model how to gracefully and graciously receive the knowledge, wisdom, values and collectively the culture of generations past, and carry them into the future - molding and evolving these understanding to the needs of the day.

If the line is successful, I will find myself in a similar position that Walt finds himself in today - attempting to guide passionate young people towards a life of meaning and value. Luckily I have his example to work from, and hopefully the generations after me will be able to make good use of the example I helped to model.

Questions and Conclusions

We went to Windward looking for answers to our questions about how a line family could work. We had some specific questions that got answered. But mostly we found answers to questions that we had not thought to ask. You have now read the thoughts and ideas from Windward members. It is up to you to make of these ideas what you will.

When our weekend at Windward was over we reviewed our most basic questions. Did we find all the answers? Many, but not all and we did find some better questions. We asked many of those new questions at other communities that we visited. Did we find perfection? No but we found a system that is working well and is working to get better. Is Windward the only, or ultimate, line family model? We believe a line family can take many forms and that people must find their own paths. Did we find hope? Yes! We found enthusiasm, spirit and love; the love of community and the adventure of finding a new and perhaps better path. We found people on an adventure looking for - and finding - a new life and new meaning.

Most of all we found inspiration. No one at Windward expects their life to be easy, but they expect it to be interesting, fun and challenging. And these are the things, in our humble opinion, that make life worth living.

Elon's Opinion on the Windward Line Family

They are awesome! Richard and I were so thrilled when he discovered that there is at least one line family out there, and that it had been ongoing for 30 years! And we were again excited when they agreed to write something for our book, and amazed at what a wonderful job they did of expressing themselves! I guess all the exclamation points tell you what I think about this group of people. It isn't easy inventing everything from scratch, which is sort of what the Windward group did, and what they continue to do to this day. My hat is off to them!

Our deepest fear is not that we are inadequate. Our deepest fear is that we are powerful beyond measure. It is our light, not our darkness that most frightens us.

M. Williamson

It was in 1992 that Deborah Anapol's seminal book on polyamory, Love Without Limits was first published. Its arrival was perfectly timed for Richard, his partner and their mutual friends, a married couple. Richard and his partner had known them since their early days together in public school. They were discovering that mutual attractions were developing between the two couples, which extended beyond their long-term friendships. It was then that Richard heard Deborah on a local radio station giving an interview about her book. He immediately went out and purchased it and read it in a couple of days. He then bought three more copies for his partner and their friends. Deborah's book gave them permission to explore their relationships in ways they had not really considered possible.

We wrote this book to give you and your family permission to explore new territory. We have found that the science fiction notion of non-monogamy works. Now let's find out how well the science fiction lifestyle of the line family works. The Windward line family has already proved that people with a similar vision can work together and develop dreams into realities.

We leave you with one last quote that must be true for most authors. It certainly strikes a chord with us:

> *One always has a better book in one's mind than one*
> *can manage to get onto paper.*

Michael Cunningham

We will feel extremely successful if this book inspires people to explore the possibilities that living as a line family has to offer. We invite you to keep in touch with us and let us know how you are doing. Become our teachers by letting us know what you discover so that we can pass it on in new editions of the book and in future online resources. We are always open to, and welcome, constructive suggestions and new information about what you have discovered and how your line family is doing.

We want a dialog with our readers. You can contact us at: director@line-family.info.

We wish you the best of love, abundance and belonging.

ABOUT THE AUTHORS

Richard Gilmore is a long-time polyamory activist, researcher and writer. His primary research is on poly family economics, group decision making and non-sexual intimacy. As the vice president of Polycamp NW he was a charter member of the board of directors for the first 10 years. Richard was also the host of Seattle's Poly Potluck. He joined Elon and her husband Jim, over 14 years ago, to form a triad that quickly grew to a quad with in addition of Jim's girlfriend Judy to the family.

Elon de Arcana's two primary interests in line families are economies of scale and having a date on New Year's Eve. From a young age, she has questioned the reasonableness of every small family group needing to own all of the tools needed to run a household. Along with physical resources, Elon questioned why humans did not share emotional resources, aka love, more freely. She has found that the line family model addresses economic and emotional issues very well.

Elon and Richard have given their line family presentation across the country from Maui to upstate New York, at polyamorous meetups, science fiction conventions and private homes. They would love to be invited to come speak to, and with, your group.

www.ingramcontent.com/pod-product-compliance
Lightning Source LLC
Chambersburg PA
CBHW052032090426
42739CB00010B/1874